Foundations for Fund-raising

CW01090951

Other titles in the Charities Management series:

Foundations for Fund-raising

Redmond Mullin

Published in association with the Institute of Chartered
Secretaries and Administrators

First published 1995 by
ICSA Publishing Limited
Campus 400, Maylands Avenue
Hemel Hempstead
Hertfordshire HP2 7EZ

Typeset in 10/12.5pt Palatino
by Columns Design and Production Services Ltd, Reading

Printed and bound in Great Britain by Biddles Ltd, Guildford and
King's Lynn

British Library Cataloguing in Publication Data

A catalogue record for this book is available from
the British Library
ISBN 1-872860-73-7 (pbk)

1 2 3 4 5   99 98 97 96 95

To my friends and mentors in fund-raising: Frank Wells, Bill Aramony, Harold Sumption; and in advertising: John Treasure and David Curling; and to good fund-raisers everywhere.

Quas dederis solas semper habebis opes
You own forever the wealth you give away

Martial, *Epigrams*, Book V, XLII

Contents

Series editor's foreword

In the United States a considerable body of academic literature has been presented which identifies the voluntary sector as a distinct area of study. There has also been an outpouring of books on 'best practice' and 'how to do it'.

In the United Kingdom we currently do not enjoy this depth of academic research; instead we have a few pockets of academic researchers. In addition there are a limited number of texts outlining best practice, ranging from small factual briefing notes that are soon outdated to large professional 'information texts'.

I believe the United Kingdom needs a series of quality books that will move beyond the 'handbook' while providing practical advice – a series that will offer a strong grounding of theoretical debate and pragmatic analysis.

This series attempts to fulfil that need. Written by a multidisciplinary team of academics and practitioners, the series aims to breach the gap between theoretical texts and practical guides. We have sought to explore and identify the specific characteristics of the voluntary sector, thus enabling those working either in or with that sector to fulfil their tasks more effectively.

Paul Palmer

Foreword

Fund-raising is not just about asking for money. It is not begging. Of course, money is a key part of the fund-raising process, indeed the measure by which fund-raising and fund-raisers are judged. But the fund-raising process should not start with money.

In the 1980s, fund-raising became increasingly 'professional'. The emphasis was on technique and technology, and a generation of fund-raisers emerged who were highly skilled in 'segmentation', 'response rates', 'telemarketing' and 'merchandising'. Attracting new donors was 'increasing the size of the database'. The donor got lost.

However, the 1990s is the age of consumer choice. The average Sainsbury's store has 15,000 lines. Companies talk about customer care and consumer charters. The emphasis is on putting the customer first. So, increasingly, the successful fund-raiser is the one who understands the essential relationship between donor and cause, and sees donors as partners in meeting the need. What motivates them to give? What are *their* needs and aspirations in the relationship? What involvement and recognition do they want or expect? How do they relate to each other? The role of the fund-raiser is to build real, meaningful relationships that satisfy the donor, as well as to optimise income for the cause.

Redmond Mullin has a unique understanding of this model of fund-raising. As anyone who has met him will testify, his physical stature masks an even greater intellect. After periods as an academic, a practising Jesuit and a senior executive with advertising agency J. Walter Thompson, Redmond brought his analytical mind to the process of fund-raising, studying its history, writing about it and practising it.

No one in this country today has done more for the development of fund-raising. While at the Charities Aid Foundation, he created and launched *Charity Statistics*, now *Charity Trends*, and ran the *Directory of Grant-Making Trusts* – both of which are now standard references. It was at a meeting between Redmond and the appeals directors of some of the major charities that he sowed the seeds of what became the Institute of Charity Fund-raising Managers. It is appropriate that, as well as becoming vice-chairman for a period, he was also chairman of its fund-raising and training committees in its early years. He pioneered prospect research for fund-raising in setting up Anderida as a subsidiary of his company, Redmond Mullin Ltd. He wrote several books and articles. And he worked with his clients to raise hundreds of millions of pounds.

This combination of practice, historical study and rigorous intellectual analysis has given Redmond a profound understanding of the nature of the fund-raising relationship. Ken Burnett, in his seminal book *Relationship Fundraising*, approached this from the perspective of the direct mail donor. Redmond approaches it from the perspective of a major donor to a one-off appeal. The motivations of the two kinds of donor may be different, but the principles are the same.

This book is the quintessence of Redmond's analysis and experience. He explains the theories and he shows how organisations, including mine, have made theory reality. He explores what it is that will cause a donor to give a 'major gift' – major, that is, in relation to the potential of the donor.

Concepts such as the 'fund-raising cycle' seem to belong to Redmond. Yet, as he himself demonstrates, they were being used in the Middle Ages and before. He articulates them in a way that seems obvious, yet his notions are profound. They could be dismissed with a cursory 'of course' – or they could change the way we *think* about fund-raising, the way we structure our organisations and the way we behave tomorrow! (Redmond's 'fund-raising cycle' is now used as the basis for the ICFM foundation course in fund-raising and to structure the entire National Fundraisers' Convention.)

Although the principles in this book are written with the one-off appeal in mind, they apply equally to the whole strategy of a charity raising £40 million a year, the organisation of a simple coffee morning or an appeal to repair the local church roof.

When I started work with Redmond in 1980 on the NSPCC's centenary, the notion of a £12 million appeal for a charity of this kind was considered as outrageously ambitious. Our success in achieving £15 million paved the way for ever larger appeals, like the Wishing Well Appeal. Our success was, in very large measure, due to Redmond's continued (and often irritating) insistence on the rigorous application of his principles.

This introduction may sound like a eulogy. It is not meant to be – rather, an encouragement. Please read what follows carefully. It is short, but not short on ideas. It is dense and tersely written. It is complete and self-contained. It may seem theoretical at times. But its distillation provides frameworks and tools which all of us involved in planning fund-raising can operate in a genuinely practical way.

And in the end it just seems like common sense.

Giles Pegram

Preface

This short book brings together a number of papers I have given and adds blocks of new material, covering some basic principles for fund-raising. It is intended as a guide and stimulus at all points of experience and practice: when starting out in fund-raising; when planning a total or special fund-raising strategy; when resolving a problem. It is relevant for fund-raising of all kinds. The emphasis here is on *major support*: where the units of support sought and achieved are high in relation to the funding requirements and to the supporters' potential. In other words, the fund-raising is designed to secure a high proportion of the target from a few sources only, and these sources may be targeted for multiples of thousands rather than hundreds of pounds. The principles apply to all forms of support – gifts or grants, sponsorships or promotions, employee activity, events or functions – separately or in combination. I shall explain this at several points throughout the text.

The following topics are dealt with in sequence:

- An outline history of professional fund-raising from the first century to today, providing a context and background for present practice.
- The characteristics of the not-for-profit sector and the roles and status of fund-raising within it.
- A fundamental discipline: the fund-raising *cycle* and its applications.
- Leadership, process and communications.
- A dynamic for fund-raising: an increasing returns model applied to a series of cases.

People say they want examples of successful (and unsuccessful) appeals, not theory. Without sound theory such anecdotes cannot be analysed and good models or analogies cannot be applied to new situations. The theoretical parts of this book have been applied to deliver hundreds of millions of pounds for my clients and others who have used these principles. I make no apology for theory which creates understanding of success and failure, opening the way for better future performance.

There are several people to be thanked. Elisabeth Seince (who is my conscience and free will in business affairs) typed the changing manuscript and helped and advised on the text. My old friend John Stockdale, who, when at Mowbrays in 1976, published my *Fundraising Handbook*, acted as my agent and adviser for this book. Giles Pegram wrote the Foreword and encouraged the enterprise. He also read the manuscript and contributed, with his staff, to the NSPCC case study. I drew on David Cook's 1991 paper from ICFM's Birmingham Convention for the NIVT case study, to which he and Paul Sweeney contributed extensively. Sir Harold Haywood, Harold Sumption, Ken Burnett, Rob Paton and Stephen Lee were other readers of the manuscript who gave their comments to me. Finally, this book has been yet another distraction from family life. So I thank Greg, Caedmon, Frankie, Ben and Sebastian but above all Carol for their long-suffering forbearance.

Redmond Mullin

1 Two thousand years of disreputable history

Chapter summary

Charities and the fund-raising that supports their activities have been established for over 2,000 years. Both originally drew on Jewish and Graeco-Roman traditions. Fund-raising throughout its history has depended on leaders, volunteers and a range of methods segmented in relation to target supporters. The principles have remained constant although activity has been affected by circumstances and by the means available – pulpit or television. It seems there have almost always been professional fund-raisers and that criticism of them has remained fairly constant, hence 2,000 years of regulation and licensing. Today we are in a period of extraordinary competition, with national and international regulation a crucial topic.

Fund-raising in late antiquity

There is famine in Palestine; give your support. I am sending Titus to receive the money you promised and have told people how generous you will be. Every week before he arrives, set aside a considered sum, calculated according to your means. It must be ready before I get there, so that there is no fund-raising during my visit. If you are not as generous as you promised to be, I and you will be shamed. There were previous complaints about the handling of funds, so please appoint trustees to account for the money and to take it to Jerusalem. If you like, I will go with them.

That is a paraphrase of part of Paul's letters to the Corinthians, promoting famine relief to Palestine, written less than thirty years after the Crucifixion.[1]

Paul's is a remarkable precedent for fund-raising letters. It is also part of one of the greatest – perhaps *the* greatest – world traditions of fund-raising and community care. These early Christians were continuing a Jewish tradition which survives today. Then it was common practice for the Jews of the diaspora to send funds to Jerusalem, even after its destruction in AD 70. As late as the third century, fund-raisers were being appointed to organise this activity.[2]

That was only one aspect of Jewish fund-raising and charity. There were people in each community assigned to fund-raising; others to the distribution of food, clothes and funds. Rabbi Jose ben Halafta prayed for the job of fund-raiser to avoid the distributor's hard choices. Rabbi Akiba said: 'It is a greater virtue to cause another to give than to give yourself', blessing fund-raisers. Giving was assessed proportionately to means (as Paul suggests) with the object that no member of the community and no visiting Jew should be in need.[3] Care embraced the *ger*, the gentile resident, the non-Jew.[4] As we have seen, it included relief and alms for Jerusalem. The tradition continued and developed over the following centuries. In the sixteenth, seventeenth and eighteenth centuries meal and lodging tickets were being used in Europe as part of a community-chest-style operation, to do away with the humiliation of begging. As in Paul's collection, funds for meal tickets were raised in proportion to a household's means. Regulations in Franconia in 1765 said that 'the cantor is to apportion [contributions] properly and impartially so that the poorer [citizens] do not have too heavy a burden and the richer do not have too few meals to supply'.[5] Such extraordinary systematic generosity continues in contemporary Jewish communities, for their own needs, for Israel and for goyim.

The European fund-raising tradition was already drawing on established structures and practice from its beginning. It drew on the traditions – Roman and Greek – of the Roman Empire as well as on Judaism. Much in that sophisticated world seems familiar. The rich man of Gytheion who, in AD 161–9, gave oils for the baths, did so on condition that three marble pillars publicising his philanthropy be set up at the most prominent places in town. So, in the twelfth century, Bubwith of Wells provided 160 craftsmen's salaries on condition that the north tower be named after him.[6] So, today, the name on a building or facility can clinch a gift. Indeed in the ancient world the funding of public works and social service by the very rich sometimes took the place of taxation. Private gifts often funded civil works, public buildings, poor relief and even the fleet, as well as circuses and public display.[7]

It seems that the early Christian communities, like their Jewish neighbours around the Mediterranean, provided for themselves and generously for others. They too made donations through a kind of community chest from which everyone, especially the poorest, benefited.[8] Christian religion was more than paying its way. Meanwhile, there was organised fund-raising for the pagan temples (which had also provided for the poor). During the first century a committee was set up to organise charity sales and collections for the temple at Lindos. Donors' names could be inscribed on still-vacant statue bases and plaques.[9] Some Christians mocked the pagans for this, perhaps complacent about their own self-sufficiency: Tertullian (about AD 187) wrote 'Let Jupiter hold out his hand for alms!'[10]

Those pagan temples enjoyed valuable tax concessions and benefited from considerable endowments as well as from income-earning assets such as shops and breweries. Despite Tertullian's mockery, Christians eventually sought benefit from these and, under Constantine, received them. In 373 Basil (Bishop of Caesarea), a knowing manipulator of the state system, who had set up a large hostel and hospice outside Caesarea about a year before, wrote to the Imperial Prefect's Assistant: 'have the kindness to inspect the home for the poor … and exempt it entirely from taxation … to make the small property of the poor immune from assessment'.[11] It was an important (and corrupting) moment for the new religion when Constantine removed distribution of poor relief – in bread and corn doles – from pagan to Christian priests. Even by Basil's time, founding donors' names and portraits were appearing on Christian buildings and by 321 there was a large flow of legacies to the Christian church and its causes. Peter Brown writes: 'the ancient search for personal fame through well-publicised giving, had entered the church in a peculiarly blatant form'.[12]

The fund-raising and giving of the Christian churches reached far away: in 253 Cyprian in Carthage sent 100,000 sesterces to devastated Numidia; and the church in Rome cared for 1,500 indigent people, many of them refugees. Ambrose in Milan sent ransoms for prisoners in the Balkans (selling his Arian enemies' memorial patens and chalices to pay for this).[13] So the Emperor Julian, in the early 360s, who tried to turn the tide and restore the empire to paganism, complained: 'No Jew is ever begging and the impious Galileans [Christians] support not only their poor but ours as well.'[14] He was, as a pagan, wise. Support of the poor through its charity was to give the strengthening church distinctive influence as the late Roman Empire (West and East) christianised itself. The poor, disregarded by non-Christian communities, became a special factor for the churches', and particularly their bishops', successful bid for power. Among the poor, then as now, lone parents and the homeless were particularly abandoned. The poor without status were a threat in the growing cities. The bishops and churches embraced them, thus offering security to the state and securing their own statutory position. As numbers of the indigent grew, the church listed the approved poor and, after the Council of Chalcedon, issued under a bishop's signature their licences for begging – a practice that was to become familiar again in pre- and post-Reformation Europe.[15]

Much of that early fund-raising was managed by people within the Christian (or Jewish) community assigned to this task. Were there professionals as well as volunteers? Perhaps. In Eusebius's (260–340) *Ecclesiastical History*, the heretic Montanus is criticised because 'It is he . . . who appointed collectors of money, who organised the receiving of gifts under the name of offerings. . .'[16] If this is the professionals' first appearance in history, it is in a hostile text – something you will be used to by the end of this chapter.

Fund-raising in the Middle Ages

I regard the term 'Dark Ages', describing the period following the first Christian era, of which I have given a thumbnail sketch above, as a misleading generalisation; but Gildas, a British monk perhaps writing from South Wales about 540 or from the South of England about 500, certainly saw darkness around him, after

Roman withdrawal from our island about AD 420. One feature of that darkness is the collapse of Christian charity: the clergy 'regard the honourable poor as snakes, and cultivate the wicked rich; they say with their lips that alms should be given, but give not a halfpenny themselves'.[17]

With a leap, we are in the Middle Ages, a definitive time for charities. It was during this period that trust law was established in Britain. During the thirteenth century, the Franciscan order was founded. Its elected poverty prevented not just its members but also the order itself from ownership of property. To allow gifts to reach the friars, a 'spiritual friend' outside the order owned and managed property on the friars' behalf. This was – according to the constitutional historian F.W. Maitland – the origin of our trust law.[18]

This was also the period during which those famous 'heads of charity' from the 1601 Act were gradually formulated. During the Middle Ages they were a statement of priorities for benevolent action and for funding, to which spiritual benefits would be attached as an incentive. They identified the private and communal issues towards which voluntary funding should be directed. This is why roads, bridges and causeways sit in religious tracts and legal instruments beside the building of churches and care for the sick and the poor. Langland (poet laureate for the poor and disabled), writing between 1360 and 1370, cites as objects for charity hospitals, the unfortunate, the sick, bad roads, broken bridges, help for maidens, the bedridden poor, prisoners, sending young children to school and the endowment of religion. The same objects for charity occurred before and after Langland, in preaching textbooks and lists of the works of mercy, and only gradually in enabling legislation – which was often intended to correct abuse, to reduce pressure on public authorities and to limit liability on a town or community regarding vagrants and sturdy beggars, particularly when large numbers of discharged soldiers and sailors were roaming the country, jobless at the end of a war.[19]

This was also a high period for fund-raising. In 1174, when the monastery of St Evurtius, just outside the walls of Orleans, had been sacked by the Normans, Bishop Stephan sent out two fund-raising letters, parts of which I paraphrase: 'Standing in the smoking ashes of our church among the scorched timbers of its walls, soon to rise again, we are forced to approach the general public and shamelessly to ask for support from outside gifts.'[20]

Fund-raising developed great sophistication during the Middle Ages. Table 1.1 shows an analysis of fund-raising for Troyes Cathedral between 1389 and 1423. I have selected clusters of support to illustrate particular points.

Appeals refer to professionally staffed campaigns organised in the region around Troyes. The staff were professional fund-raisers. The three named were John of Villette, William and Theobald. I shall come back to them; but note that, for security as well as from devotion, boxes from these appeals were opened publicly each year on the day of the Great Synod. *Legacies* I shall not discuss; but *Citizens* refers to the people of Troyes itself, in their various social and economic orders. *Big gifts* refers to very large sums from rich individual sources, described below. *Other* is a huge category. It includes, varying year by year, relics, collecting boxes, special masses, community associations and many other categories.

Consider some interesting features of these records. Why did citizens' contributions surge in 1390–1? Because the nave fell down and they wanted to preserve their cathedral. Why did appeals (the regional, professionally managed appeals) collapse by 1422? Because the Battle of Agincourt was fought a few miles away in 1415, leaving the countryside impoverished. (The 1420 Treaty of Troyes settled the conflict and Henry V's marriage to Catherine.) Why did the big gifts fluctuate? This was a common pattern with cathedral appeals. The main donors at Troyes were:

Table 1.1 Troyes Cathedral fund-raising, Agincourt period, in pounds

	1389–90	1390–1	1412–13	1422–3
Appeals	176 (17%)	186 (13%)	160 (15%)	34 (6%)
Legacies	44 (4%)	5 (4%)	54 (5%)	22 (4%)
Citizens	29 (3%)	386 (28%)	40 (4%)	70 (7%)
Big gifts	440 (43%)	250 (18%)	100 (9%)	100 (17%)
Other	331 (32%)	572 (41%)	695 (66%)	380 (66%)
Total	1,020	1,399	1,049	606

Note: Percentage figures are rounded up or down, and may not add up to 100%.
Source: Adapted from Stephen Murray, *Building of Troyes Cathedral*, Indiana, 1987.

in 1389, £300 from the chapter, £40 from the bishop, £100 from the Duke of Burgundy; in 1390–1, £200 from King Charles V and £50 from the Pope; in 1412–13, £100 from the Duke of Burgundy (assassinated 1419 – see Shakespeare); in 1422–3, £100 from the new Duke of Burgundy.[21]

For a more detailed description of medieval fund-raising, Table 1.2 shows the segmentation of giving between sources, methods used and motivations for the building of Milan Cathedral between 1386 and 1391.

That remarkable campaign was described in an article published by Edmund Bishop at Downside in 1899. He describes how the community came together productively at every level to achieve their cathedral. It was a few individuals who started the street and house-to-house collections. It was civic rivalry between guilds and fraternities and between other classes and groups in Milan which brought out the volunteer teams. The fund-raising was managed by a committee. There really were jumble sales and schools fund-raising. There was also an admirable attempt at major support fund-raising. Here is

Table 1.2 Milan Cathedral fund-raising, 1386–91

Source	Method and purpose	Motivations
Very rich individual	Request for marker gift To ask and be model for the rich	Memorial Salvation
Rich individuals (nobles, soldiers, lawyers, doctors)	Request for major support Pressure from Court Legacies Sons' volunteer labour Committee membership	Memorials Salvation Peer esteem
Prosperous individuals	Through confraternities Sponsor craftsmen, navvies Gifts in kind Legacies Committee membership	(Memorial) Salvation Peer group Citizenship
Ordinary people	House-to-house collections Street collections Fund-raising events and functions Jumble sales Volunteer labour	Salvation Peer group Citizenship
Young	Schools fund-raising	

part of the letter sent by the appeal presidents to their main prospect, the Conte de Virtu, asking

That you and the illustrious Ladies, your lady mother and the wife and the daughter of your Lordship, would deign to send hither by such persons as you think proper, your devout offerings in aid of the building fund, and recommend your officials and the persons attached to your court to join also in the good work; for soldiers, and lawyers, and doctors, in a word the nobles of your said city of Milan, will be all ready to offer along with them, to the intent that the Almighty, who rewards a hundredfold those who give for his sake, may preserve and happily increase your good estate. Notifying also to your Highness that if your pious and devout oblations are thus forthcoming, an arcading of the aforesaid church can in a very short time be finished, and a marble tomb, in which it has been already determined that the bones of the Magnificent Lord, your father, of good and happy memory, should rest, can be placed honourably under it.[22]

We know what happened in those cathedral appeals from the very detailed Fabric Books, where they have survived (the 'Fabric' referred to the building). Even then Friends of the Fabric organisations were very active. The Fabric Books tell us, at Exeter for example, where the stone came from, who shipped and carried it, who carved it, who applied the gold leaf and colour – and what all these cost. The Fabric Books also tell how the funds to do all this were raised.[23]

There was uniformity, apparently, in fund-raising around Europe in the Middle Ages. Where there was a peculiar social structure this was reflected in the fund-raising, as at Strasburg, where the citizens controlled their city and the building of its cathedral. These were some of the ways in which the funds were raised:

- Collection boxes, common since antiquity, occur everywhere. Poor Friar Elias, succeeding St Francis and cast as a Judas figure, is criticised for installing one on the site of the basilica he was building in Assisi, in 1230, to hold the saint's body.
- It was very usual for there to be matching funding between bishop and chapter for building their cathedral, the chapter perhaps pledging 50 per cent of the bishop's commitment (as, for example, at Exeter and Chartres).
- There was high-society fund-raising: at New Sarum, in 1220, noblemen and noblewomen could lay a foundation stone,

then covenant a seven-year subscription to the fabric fund.

- There were many major patrons. Bishop Thoresby (between 1352 and 1373) at York funded 650 salaries for the minster. Bishop Grandisson at Exeter was helping to fund both his cathedral and his bridge (still visible) about 1328. There were foundations by kings and queens. Henry III and Henry VII made major foundations. Nobles such as Henry de Blois were involved: he set up one of England's most ancient charities at St Cross, Winchester. There were merchants such as Gervase of Southampton, who founded God's House and endowed it as a hospital for poor folk there.
- There was endowment through income-earning assets such as shops, markets, mineral assets, fisheries and mills (cf. current charity trading). Thus in the twelfth century the cathedral chapter was co-owner of the Great Quay in Amiens. Dues levied on Jewish families and enterprises might be transferred to a church or monastery. In Barcelona in the fourteenth century income from the mills was intended to secure income for the hospital there, relieving it of dependence on small-scale fund-raising.
- There are even records of sponsored bell-ringing at Rouen and in other places.[24]

The guilds were powerful vehicles for medieval, communal philanthropy. They were formed for various purposes: for piety, to mount miracle plays, and most enduringly as mutual-help associations within a craft or trade. That last form of association has survived in the City of London and other livery companies. More pious types of guild were abolished at the Reformation. Guilds were the original community-chest bodies. There were real, wooden, iron-bound chests, often with strong double locks, which could only be opened by two aldermen with separate keys. Guildsmen looked after each other and their families, visiting the sick (perhaps with a bottle from the guild's ale store) and providing grants and pensions. There was assistance with grants and loans at times of financial difficulty. All guilds had benevolent objects written into their statutes and looked for contributions, sometimes apportioned according to means, from members. The statutes of a York guild declared: 'Vain is the gathering of the faithful unless some work of kindliness is done.' Most guilds were also committed to works of mercy for non-members and to altruistic objects: poor, sick and handicapped people; travellers; schools and schoolmasters; roads, bridges and causeways.[25] We have seen how the guilds of a city might rally to the building of their cathedral, as in Milan and more potently at Strasburg. Indeed, in Strasburg, the guilds had crucial welfare roles. There was overlap across Europe between guild activity and the systematisation of relief and statutory limitation to a community's responsibility for relief. The intention of much Tudor legislation is simultaneously reflected in the sixteenth-century *Aumone Générale* in France. There was a common box and an official collector. There was assessment and listing of the needy. Tokens entitling holders to relief were issued. They even calculated that a man needed one and a half pounds of bread daily. It was forbidden to give alms outside this system.[26] In Britain the 1536 Beggar's Act threatened penalties for unsystematic philanthropy:

no manner of person . . . shall give any ready money in alms, otherwise than to the common boxes and common gatherings . . . upon pain to lose and forfeit ten times the value of all such ready money as shall be given in alms contrary to the tenor and purport of [the Act].

This was an early attempt at the control of giving and of relief.[27]

There was also professional fund-raising. The professionals were called *quaestores eleemosynarii*: seekers of alms. They mounted *quests* – campaigns or appeals – for funds. We know them largely through the satire of Langland and Chaucer, the ordinances to control them, and complaints from bishops on the one hand and Lollards with other reformers on the other hand against their abuses. The *quaestores* included Langland's and Chaucer's pardoners.[28]

They were conspicuously successful, hence the real corruption and the criticism. The 1215 Lateran Council decreed that *quaestores* could only operate under licence from their bishop or from the Pope, a formula already guaranteed to stir strife where papal demands for funds were unwelcome. Despite the regulations, the *quaestores'* success attracted fraud. False fund-raisers (sometimes brought in by the chapter) would mount appeals, for their own and sometimes the chapter's gain. Grandisson complained about it. Thoresby uttered against it: the fraudulent fund-raisers would be 'cursed in every act of living and blotted out of the Book of the Living' – if they did not return the cash they had raised.[29]

Fraud and personal gain were, perhaps, the least damaging criticisms of the *quaestores*. What they offered was the purchase of salvation. The enticement for giving offered by that good Bishop Stephan at Orleans was a visit by the saints' relics. Relics would be taken on tour or, if they would not travel, could be visited at home. St Firmin's relics at Amiens miraculously refused to leave the city in 1137, attracting many pilgrims to the town, benefiting its and the church's economies. (Pilgrims determined much church architecture, even into this century.) The relics of St Firmin were said to raise (*gaigner*) the funds. Why? Because they could provide remission from the pains of purgatory for oneself or for a nominee, a concession introduced by Urban II in 1095 to promote his crusade, in return for a visit, a payment, or usually both.[30]

It was salvation purchased through gifts that these medieval fund-raisers offered, to their own, their licence-givers' and notionally the donors' gains. They bore relics and were probably the first laymen allowed into Christian pulpits. Langland's pardoner preached 'as if he were a priest'. They drew wrath from reformers as well as satire from poets. They could work for a variety of causes. Chaucer's swindling, prospering pardoner raised funds for the hospital of the Blessed Mary of Rouncivalle near Charing Cross.

Fund-raising after the Reformation

On 31 October 1517 the Pope's arch fund-raiser, the Dominican John Tetzel, came to sell indulgences near Wittenberg. He was raising money for building St Peter's in Rome and to help pay off a huge debt owed by Prince Bishop Albert of Brandenburg to the Fuggers, who were massive money-lenders. The family still has charitable foundations in Europe. At Wittenberg, Prince Frederick the Wise of Saxony had built up his own collection of relics, from which he wanted to see profits. Far more potently, Martin Luther was Professor of Scripture there. When the Saxons flooded across the border to hear Tetzel preach and to pay for pardons and remissions, Luther protested against such purchase of paradise by publishing his ninety-five theses.[30] His was the cause of salvation by faith alone.

Of course the criticism did not begin with Luther; nor did the debate end with him. Yet it was the *quaestor* or fund-raiser Tetzel who sparked the Reformation. (In recognition, the American *Philanthropy Monthly* makes its annual Tetzel Award to the most discreditable fund-raising performance each year.)

Roman indulgences were peddled on into our own time; but what was left for the Protestant world? With promises of salvation abandoned, the main elements of technique and leadership could stay in place. Reflect back from today's media for mass communication – television, radio, press – and think where coverage, intensity and effectiveness could be achieved in England during the sixteenth and seventeenth centuries. The pulpit was a medium through which most people could be reached, week by week. It had been the medium for the pardoners before the Reformation. Now it was used as potently. In 1536, the year in which he issued his Act Against Papal Authority, Henry VIII also decreed in his Beggars' Act that 'every preacher, parson, vicar, curate of the realm' should use sermons and all other means to 'exhort, move, stir and provoke people to be liberal and bountifully to extend their . . . alms and contributions . . . toward the comfort and relief of . . . poor, impotent, decrepit, indigent and needy people'.[31]

Henry VIII did not give the first example. Henry III, among others, had been there before him. Reformed monarchs became regular fund-raisers for such causes as the Society for the Propagations of the Gospel. Queen Anne, George I, George II, George III, George IV, William IV and Queen Victoria all wrote appeal letters on its behalf. Listen to George III (mad, loser of North America, 'What George? What Third?' of Byron's *Vision of Judgement*): 'upon this occasion, Ministers in each parish [are to] effectually excite their parishioners to a liberal contribution' which would be collected at their homes during the following week by the church wardens and overseers for the poor.[32]

Royal patronage and the pulpit were only one aspect of fund-raising in England after Henry VIII. Printing was a main instrument of Reformation. Print and literacy increased in influence. Here is a direct marketing appeal by the Quaker John

Bellers in his *Proposals for Raising a College of Industry* (the origin of the Saffron Walden Boarding School) in 1696. He is itemising the needs in what looks like an excellent appeal:

For every 300 persons, the raising of:
£10,000 to buy an Estate in Land of £500 p.a.
£2,000 to Stock the Land
£3,000 to prepare Necessaries to Set the Several Trades to Work
£3,000 For New-building or Repairing Old
In all 18,000 pound
An hundred pound a year in such a College, I suppose will maintain ten times as many people as £100 a year in alms-houses. . .[33]

By 1712 the Society for Promoting Christian Knowledge (SPCK) and others were beginning to build their residing and subscribing members lists, their databases of supporters. Some of the subscribers' rights were, to modern sensibility, worrying: the Royal Hospital and Home for Incurables (now the Royal Home at Putney) was a 'voting charity'. Your donation allowed you to cast votes which determined who would be admitted.[34] At Christ's Hospital school, sharing its founder with the Royal Hospital and Home for Incurables, similar rights exist today.

Restrictions such as licensing persisted. In 1718 'a little contingent' from St Anne's, Aldersgate, arrived without licence to raise funds in Chislehurst. They were brought before the High Sheriff. He demanded: 'By what right are you strolling and begging through the country without a licence?' One of the trustees was sent to gaol.[35]

All the time, social leadership dominated large segments of English fund-raising. Subscription lists for charities were sometimes headed by William III, Queen Anne or Queen Victoria.[36] Hogarth and Handel devotedly raised funds for the Foundling Hospital – Handel was anxious for those children even on his death bed.[37] There was great concern and generosity – and vulgarity: 'Find a Duchess, flatter her and get £500' was the motto of the *Press Bazaar News* late in the nineteenth century.[38]

Where were the 'professionals'? As usual, they emerge in criticism – from Pepys (devoted to Christ's Hospital) and others because of the percentage that professional companies were taking. In the eighteenth and nineteenth centuries, companies like Robert Hodgson & Byrd and Hall & Stevenson were taking 5–7.5 per cent of the sums raised.[39]

Modern fund-raising

Professionally designed and managed fund-raising of the kind I practise probably started about 1883, in the United States, for the Young Men's Christian Association (YMCA). That was the beginning of a new style of professionalism. In 1919 Ward, Hill, Pierce and Wells became the first professional fund-raising company of its kind, Wells having previously worked for the YMCA. After moving to Australia and New Zealand, Frank Wells and his father came to England. From their activity emerged two other main fund-raising companies, Craigmyle and Hooker, both with principal staff trained by Wells in the Antipodes. From these came a highly trained generation of professionals.[40] Had my colleague Martin lived, he would in 1992 have transformed the company from Wells, Mullin to Stroud, Wells, Mullin, continuing that tradition into another century.

During the late 1950s and early 1960s, about the time that the Wells company was transforming some aspects of fund-raising, a revolution emerged. The issue was the Third World. Before that period, Third World causes had relatively weak impact, except for occasional appeals, often associated with church missionary initiatives, and sometimes combining Christian with imperial expansion.[41] Then independence for North African nations, World Refugee Year and famine in Biafra and the Congo created an impetus which gave their cause priority. Photographs of starving children and adults in the poor world shocked our rich world into its response. For the rest of the century, Oxfam, War on Want, Save the Children, Christian Aid and the Catholic Fund for Overseas Development (CAFOD) would make their powerful arguments for attention, action and funding support. Simultaneously, prosperity in the West increased and a new age of consumption began in the Western democracies. New skills in communication, marketing and advertising were an essential part of that consumers' revolution, whose flowering in the United Kingdom coincided with these events.[42]

Such developments also contributed to the competition for funds which became acute from the mid-1980s onwards. Several factors created this competition. In the United Kingdom, there was rapid increase both in new charity registrations and in the number and scale of appeals launched. The full range of marketing techniques had been brought into the more sophisticated charities' fund-raising repertory. They competed through highly segmented direct marketing, sometimes controversially through telephone solicitation, and through television advertising, when this was permitted after 1990. Before the mid-1980s, major support fund-raising had largely been confined to capital appeals for universities, schools, hospitals and major arts enterprises. After the success of the National Society for the Prevention of Cruelty to Children (NSPCC), many more charities added this segment of support and style of fund-raising to their strategies. For example, there was the remarkable Wishing Well Appeal for the hospital for sick children at Great Ormond Street.[43] There were at the same time massive exercises that powerfully reached other, sometimes younger segments of the world for support: Band Aid, the Telethon and Charity Project's Comic Relief. The result was that virtually everyone was receiving better designed, higher pitched propositions for support more frequently and from more petitioners for funds than ever before.

That was one aspect of fund-raising competition. Another aspect was induced directly by government. Positively, the government liberalised the tax regime so that it encouraged more widespread and higher levels of giving. Pay As You Earn, clumsily introduced and promoted, was to encourage employees to give routinely through their payrolls. This had some impact but never delivered the implausible sums originally promised. There was also the embarrassingly titled Gift Aid, which allowed tax concessions on one-off gifts, introducing a long-needed equivalent to the tax deduction system for UK charities and donors (the latter because higher-rate taxpayers could reduce their liabilities if they used this or the covenant system). Analogous concessions had earlier been granted for companies on their one-off contributions.

At the same time government was instigating a funding crisis for most charities. New categories of indigence were being enforced by policy: for the poor, for lone-parent families and for the homeless, often with hostile propaganda against these groups to make it appear that their predicament was self-imposed. This was, for example, putting grave pressure on grant-making trusts and private or corporate philanthropists who could not see why they should provide what government had withdrawn. Meanwhile, because of government funding policies, there was sudden vast demand from established institutions and other national bodies: from the arts, from old and emergent universities and from new hospital trusts. Oxford and Cambridge universities launched appeals for targets then unprecedented here, above £250m, reaching a high proportion of UK and some other nations' establishments. For the first time in my experience there were dangers that demand would exceed supply for voluntary funding and that the country's pool of leadership for fund-raising would be exhausted.

Charities responded more constructively than simply by intensifying their fund-raising. Improvement in the quality and standards of charity personnel has been a crucial issue. There has been much to encourage this since 1980. Standards of recruitment have been raised. There have been some increases in remuneration. Training and educational provision for the sector have greatly improved, with the Open University, the London School of Economics, the South Bank and some other universities providing formal courses. Numbers of skilled people, particularly in the 30–45 age group, have grown significantly. There are emerging signs that the sector will be able to offer sound internal career progression and also some exchange with related commercial sectors. The Institute of Charity Fundraising Managers has had a crucial role in this. It has pioneered good training for charity personnel, who are still too often offered courses from other sources by people without experience or who should be disqualified by their unsuccessful performance. The Institute has introduced Codes of Conduct for a number of fund-raising activities encouraging self-regulation in this field.[44] It has had a positive impact on UK government and EU legislation and regulation; it attracts several hundred people to its annual convention. Above all, it has created a sense of professionalism in the sector, with pride in the fund-raising function.

There are still huge inadequacies in the people, institutions and resources of the charity sector. There has always been regulation, as the preceding pages have shown. Now there are dangers of excessive regulation, especially from the EU which has little knowledge or understanding of the kinds of fund-raising and charitable activity discussed in this book, just at a time when, in the United Kingdom, the sector has cooperated in the drafting of the Charity Act and has achieved a significant degree of self-regulation. There are challenges on a scale that we have never faced before. My belief in the sector is strong and my hopes for it are high. This is why, at a time made hectic by change, competition and demand, I see it as constructive to set this moment in its historic context and to propose principles for future action.

Key points

- Roles for charities and for fund-raisers are ancient.
- The principles for fund-raising have remained constant over history.
- Practice changes with context and opportunity.
- Professional fund-raisers have been involved from earliest times, and have been subject to criticism and regulation.

2 Fund-raising: values and ideals

Chapter summary

A 'charity' is *an agency which exists solely to make an adequate and relevant response to need within the community,* and this has important consequences. Needs and causes are rooted in the community; they have their own absolute priority and a relative priority depending on what the state and other agencies provide. The charitable organisation's trustees, volunteers, staff and investment must be focused on the service of need. Funders make response to need possible and through their support they share the charity's service and values. They must be kept informed and involved. Fund-raising is the function that makes responsive service possible and is as urgent as the needs served; yet the function and the people who perform it may lack esteem. To improve effectiveness, structures and procedures should bring together the people providing service, the funders and fund-raisers, and the people served, but with sensitivity and with acceptance of limits to this relationship.

What is a charity?

People and communities, values and ideals – these give life and validity to the not-for-profit sector. Fund-raising begins to go wrong when it concentrates simply on money or on the organisation itself rather than the cause and the people served.

I once defined a charity in the English sense as *an agency which exists solely to make an adequate and relevant response to need within the community.*[1] Most of the issues are still expressed there so I will use it as my starting point. There was a picture to clarify that definition (see Figure 2.1).

Need/cause

The *need* or *cause* (A in Figure 2.1) can relate to famine or poverty; to sickness or injury; to ignorance; to cultural or environmental demands – wherever there is no sufficient and affordable provision for these, either commercially or from the state.

At once that illustrates a problem with the word 'charity', which causes difficulties outside the United Kingdom, where this word or its equivalents are applied differently, or less technically. The word also causes difficulties with some types of organisation here. The term 'charity' as distinct from 'non-governmental' or 'not-for-profit' (as distinct from 'non-profit' which, the Charity Commissioners pointed out, applies to too many companies these days) is even more awkward elsewhere. Bodies regarded as 'charities' receive different fiscal and legal treatment in different nations. Universities, schools, museums, opera houses and research laboratories do not comfortably describe themselves as 'charities', yet they are caught by the definition and by 'charity' legislation which regulates and benefits them. For similar reasons, in earlier centuries, roads, bridges and causeways were

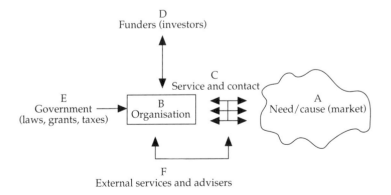

Figure 2.1

caught by such a definition and were treated as charitable objects because those urgent needs were not otherwise provided for in the community.

Needs, understanding of needs and the state's provision all change over time. This can be controversial. Charity no longer provides roads and bridges. Today there are different questions. Should opera houses be wholly or increasingly financially self-sufficient? Should grant-making trusts make good the government's inadequate provision for poor, homeless people and for lone parents? May those trusts soon be expected to pay for prescriptions, eye tests and dental care for people who can no longer afford these?

The kind of cause included here is likely to be considered urgent in itself and in relation to other causes or needs. The charity world is very competitive. It often operates irrationally. It is subject to fashion and open to influence and change. Think how much Charles Dickens or the Earl of Shaftesbury achieved in different ways in changing attitudes and the ways in which institutions cared for children, the poor and mentally disabled people. Much more recently, Mohamed Amin's BBC film report in 1984 shifted massive relief to Ethiopia. Since then, television and the media have often generated and directed the provision of aid; but the places where the film crews and journalists have been were not necessarily the most urgent and seldom the only locations of need.

Needs or causes do not float in space. They are embodied in people, communities and society. They may be located far away. Their context may be economically, culturally and socially complex: there are overlapping and often conflicting interests involved in dealing with a rainforest where the indigenous people, commercial intruders, the World Bank, various voluntary agencies and national or regional governments may have different priorities. Think of the ways in which ethnic minorities or handicapped people may be treated and represented by the agencies that serve them.

'The market' is a very flawed analogy with a cause or field of urgent need. A company may manipulate and exploit its market universes to promote profits and sales. If it does so inexpertly, it will lose its markets. The cause or field of need is what should determine and will justify the services delivered by a charity and demand both effective performance and sensitivity from all marketing and communications deployed in their support. There may be no exploitation.

The organisation

The organisation (B in Figure 2.1) may be large or small and may incorporate any or many of a variety of people: trustees and honorary associates; directing and managing staff; carers, academics, social workers, doctors, artists and arts professionals, clergy and representatives of the people served; and marketing, fund-raising and communications personnel. The organisation is likely to operate under trust law which imposes stricter responsibilities these days but can also freeze an agency's thinking, activity and responsiveness. I shall suggest how this can be avoided.

My strong point on charitable organisations is that they exist *solely* to make an adequate and relevant response to needs unmet by statutory provision. They do not exist for the comfort and glory of their trustees, directors, staff or founders. Therefore, given that needs and the provision for them by government and other voluntary agencies change over time, the organisation must ensure that:

• its understanding and description of the cause and need are still accurate and as complete as possible;
• it has taken account of any services by others responding to the same needs and has evaluated these;
• its own response is still relevant and is the best that it can provide cost-effectively and accessibly to the people it serves.

While it is legitimate for a commercial organisation – committed to showing profits for investors and motivating returns for employees – to stimulate demand in the market-place and to re-tool and redeploy if the market shifts or collapses, the options for a charity to change direction may be narrower. Yet, as with Action Research after the virtual elimination of polio or Thomas Coram in the years since the Foundling Hospital closed; or as with Relate since there was a new understanding of the issues with which it was dealing and its roles; or as with NSPCC's shifts in organisation and strategy for the protection of children – it is possible and necessary for a charity to redeploy and refocus its services consistently with its founding vision and responsively to new or newly understood needs. Where this is not possible, is there any remaining reason for a charity's survival?

Service and contact

Service and contact (C in Figure 2.1), in some cases the provision of grants, can be through staff, volunteers or both. It is artificial in most instances to separate this from the organisation itself, except that it is where sensitive, responsive service should be delivered that the organisation is to be judged. Has it the quality of skilled, sensitive and alert staff to deliver the response adequately and effectively? Does it support and train them? Is it here that improvement through increased and better directed investment is needed? This book is not the place to discuss the management of volunteers, although this and their relations with the central organisation can be crucial for the quality of service. Nor does the point apply only to welfare organisations. For example, how, when and where should universities in future deliver higher education? More fundamentally, what should be the roles and character of a university? Why and how should a health-care trust operate?

With some organisations service delivery and contacts are the responsibility of local, autonomous or effectively autonomous units structurally separated from the national body or headquarters. Some central organisations were established by their service units. Others are, sometimes nominally, in control of a federal network whose units fight for autonomy, because of local vanity and pride or because the central body is irrelevant and ineffective. Whatever the situation, the headquarters are likely to be criticised as expensive, unaware of the local issues and failing to deliver the support, the materials and the national noise needed to promote the units' activities. My immediate concern here is that failure to manage such situations will erode and may eventually invalidate the organisation's fulfilment of its mission; and that some important backers will judge an organisation by its local unit or units and prefer to support the cause through them, if they deserve this.

Funders

The funders (D in Figure 2.1) are, for this book, the second most important group, after the people served. I shall discuss their principal categories in more detail later, so here I will make some general points within the given model.

Funders are individuals, companies, trusts or foundations; singly or combined in various ways. Their first contact may come through concern about the cause, leading them to the organisation; or through the organisation alerting them to the cause; or through some other person's intervention; or by chance. Whatever type of source they represent, they are people, not chips in fund dispensers. They must therefore be persuaded to give priority to *this* cause (despite competition from others) and to decide that *this* is the best agency (despite competition) to respond to the needs.

That may sound too abstract and does not express an essential point about the people who support charities – people who are often misunderstood, neglected and occasionally despised by the staff and volunteers whose work they make possible. There are too many people in charities whose culture and ideology make them antagonistic to those other cultures that generate the surpluses, profits and wealth that must fund responsive services. The alternative is in fact incredible for a complex society and something which, on reflection, no one should want: a state that comprehensively provides all services, without contradiction or the provision of alternatives.

My positive point is that, for most funders, their financial backing of a cause is the only way that they can participate in service, and share in the vision, values and mission of the service-provider. It is not simply a transfer of funds; nor does it always end there. Given the reality of what I have stated, the more generous (relative to means) the support given, the greater the satisfaction to the supporters and the closer their identification with the cause and service organisation. Hence, the greater their motivation to continue and increase support, provided that this is permitted them.

Generous supporters want to know that they are making a valued difference; and that this can happen only if their support is given. This is why I have frequently said that fund-raising involves much more than money. Fund-raisers must understand this; which is why Frank Wells said that good fund-raisers should be generous givers.[2]

There is a last point through which I complete the picture. An investor or shareholder in a commercial company demands explicit information on performance and has direct evidence from dividends and share values on these. The supporter of a charity lacks such clear information and direct evidence but is entitled at least to something resembling them. Keeping supporters accurately and interestingly informed is a responsibility for the charity. It is also a method for keeping supporters involved and can maintain contacts so that there may be productive openness at times of difficulty. I recognise that this is not always easy. For a research charity it may be almost impossible to give a comprehensive explanation of results or projects to non-specialist supporters; but even here some explanation can be given. My point is that charities should accept their accountability to funders of all kinds and even welcome this as a means for nurturing relations with them.

I merely note here that, as in all other sectors of life, government functions as a policy-maker, partial provider of challenge funding, occasional regulator and imposer of taxes (E); and that charities, like commercial companies, use a range of external agencies from accountants and solicitors to fund-raising consultants and advertising, direct marketing and PR agencies (F).

Values and roles of fund-raising

Few charities have endowed or earned income which makes them self-sufficient. Most depend for survival or at least for development on voluntary funds secured through fund-raising. These are in most instances the means that make responsive service possible. Therefore, charity by charity, fund-raising is as valuable and urgent as the cause, the need and the services that it makes possible.

Charities and causes reach across a spectrum of values, from moral imperatives, when for example they concern poverty, famine and justice; through sympathy with some medical or disability causes; to artistic or sporting preferences. That statement is not meant to be comprehensive. My point is that the values associated with choices to support *this* or *that* charity in preference to others are of different kinds and can sometimes at rational levels be subjected to discussion and analysis. At other levels, though, precisely because this is a field of voluntary choice, such discussion and analysis is difficult: you may disagree with my choice of the local sports club or the Royal Opera House or Oxford University rather than cancer research or Amnesty or the relief of famine in Sudan, but there is little to be done if that is my preference, whether altruistic, passionate or self-interested. Nor is the choice void of value if, for example, it follows an aesthetic rather than a moral imperative or impulse.

Fund-raising's value and urgency derive from the services it makes possible and the causes served. That has important consequences. The shared values and the urgency generate a new imperative: for fund-raising professionalism. It can be a matter of justice that the people responsible for a charity's fund-raising – staff, volunteers and outside agencies – perform with the greatest skill and effectiveness. This entails responsibilities at several points: with the people directly managing the fund-raising, who must equip themselves to deliver the best attainable results with integrity; with their trustees and management, who must give them the training and resources to achieve those results and who, I argue, should equip themselves to understand and value these fund-raising functions; with the specialised staff within a charity who must understand and cooperate with the fund-raisers. Failures in terms of such responsibilities are seen where inadequate fund-raising staff scorn training; where trustees and managers hire weak staff and provide inadequate budgets and resources, giving fund-raising staff low status; where there is antagonism between fund-raising and service-delivery staff.

Over the last decade, there have been advances in the professionalism of staff, encouraged and fostered by the

Institute of Charity Fundraising Managers. Within many charities of all kinds, from welfare to arts and academic bodies, there has been greater mutual appreciation of different roles, from caring service or artistic performance to management and fund-raising, which have thus become mutually supportive and productive. However, the improvement has not been universal.

Only recently, the military director of one charity threatened funding staff because they were insisting on hearing details of the charity's development plans, on which appeals programmes should be built. There are many social-work, environmental, arts and academic charities where fund-raising is despised, sometimes but not always because failure to understand this function leads to the employment of inadequate staff. Yet funding development is not a magical function which can work remote from the service and cause.

Part of a fund-raiser's task is to argue for the function itself and for the resources that will allow it to work effectively.

Service and fund-raising: common cause

The issue is so important that I now approach it from a different point. The model we were considering included the people served; service staff and volunteers; funders and fund-raisers. There are these polarities:

1. The needy or the need: say, poverty and the poor, the homeless, tertiary education, artists and the arts, the environment.
2. The providers, responders: say, a welfare organisation, a university, an opera house, a radical campaigning group, carers, academics, social workers, arts administrators.
3. The funders and enablers: who provide the means in whatever ways, at whatever levels; or who secure the means through marketing, fund-raising, persuasion.

I recognise that there may be no separation in some organisations between points 2 and 3, and that these roles overlap; yet the *functions* are different.

Experience shows that there can be resulting tensions. Disadvantaged people may resent perceived condescension and patronage. Providers may assume power, authority and arrogance in their special expertise and skills. Funders may be patronising; or may be despised, suspected and ignored by the providers. I have seen an arts organisation describe its funding proposition as 'the sting'.[3] The enablers may be disliked by funders, held in contempt by the providers or accused of misrepresentation by the needy or those representing the need. They may actually be insensitive, inefficient or incompetent.

There could be a more liberating model in which dualities between the people involved in various ways in such voluntary enterprises were minimised and *common cause* was made between them. Of course this is an ideal. It must be designed to happen. Arrogance and manipulation by the providers and funders and misrepresentation by the enablers may impose an unproductive and demeaning separation of roles.

I propose a model which weakens dualities between parties in a voluntary enterprise (see Figure 2.2). That model reinforces some things already said, for example that there need to be open exchange and mutual respect between enablers and providers. There are some qualifications to this. There may be tensions and pressures from marketing and communications to the delivery of service and these may sometimes suggest new directions to the providers. However, marketing may not dictate a charity's service priorities nor the modes and places for service delivery. Those must be dictated by the needs. Nor, on basic issues, may the preferences of supporters determine policy or practice. On the other hand, I do not encourage rigidity. If you are a university and somebody offers £11m for archaeology you

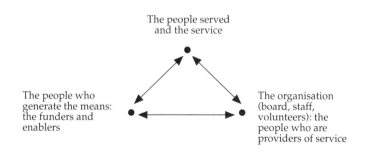

Figure 2.2

might not refuse this, although archaeology was not one of your stated priorities.

The model postulates open connections and common cause between funders, enablers and providers. This can be achieved internally through routines of briefings between departments or functions. The ways in which it can be achieved with outside funders are discussed later.

An obvious problem is the connection between funders and enablers and the people served or services themselves. Poor, sick and disabled people do not want to be gawped at by their benefactors. Funders or fund-raisers in extensive dialogue with researchers, artists and practitioners would be a nuisance. But the principle that there should be communication in both directions, where this is possible, is an important one. Most charities can offer sensitive, selective visiting. All can deliver briefings and reports on the cause and services and above all on the people who benefit. Funders can be shown how the difference that they wanted to make is being achieved.

What of communication in the other direction? With some people in acute need, the peril would be reinforcement of feelings of vulnerability and dependence. One would need to ask: what gains are there to them if they know that generosity has been directed to them? Is it awareness that people care about them? That they are not forgotten? That there are others in solidarity with them? Or is it best for the funders and providers to be silent? With other categories of people served, the issues are of a different kind. There is no harm if researchers, academics, artists or environmentalists know that they depend on voluntary support and that they have a role in securing it. Where support is on a large scale, there may be contractual obligations to give public acknowledgement, to report back and consult or to undertake joint operations.

Voluntary enterprise is generally valued in society. It is fund-raising which makes most such enterprise possible. This gives fund-raising its value and importance. It is only through their funds that most people can participate in voluntary enterprise and share the values that it embodies. This is why there should be a *continuum* between all key groups in the voluntary enterprise.

This is not a matter of abstract principle. It has crucial impact on the fund-raising. One element in the ideas used here concerns common cause and connections. *It is connections that make enterprise succeed, not the inert fixed points.* For healthy fund-raising, the connections must work in all directions.

Reprise on charities

What, briefly, should charities be? I propose that they should be the organisations that challenge and offer alternatives to existing provision; that offer responsive service where none is available. They should be organisations making a constructive difference which could not otherwise be achieved. This is also the philanthropist's aim. So charities must be vivid and relevant, not mere supplements to basically adequate statutory provision. This is why few charities should depend on statutory provision, which will threaten their efficacy and integrity. The CENTRIS report proposes a government-dependent body.[4] Such an entity would be no 'charity' by my definition, which requires the independence that comes from endowment or fund-raising, from people and institutions making voluntary provision beyond the scope of their taxes, though encouraged by some tax reliefs. Through such voluntary participation and funding they can engage with the charity in its constructive provision and its stimulus of change.

Key points

- Charities exist solely to make an adequate and relevant response to need in the community.
- This puts a responsibility for effectiveness on trustees, staff, volunteers and fund-raisers.
- Fund-raising as the enabling function is as urgent as the cause served.
- Funders participate in the values and the service through their support for a charity.
- Funders' support will be sustained and grow, the more they are informed and the greater their feeling of involvement with the charity and its values.

- There needs to be the greatest achievable common cause between the people providing services, the people who deliver the funds that make service possible and the people served.

3 The fund-raising cycle

Chapter summary

The *fund-raising cycle* is a discipline applicable to any fund-raising programme. It is a continuous process which facilitates problem analysis, planning, monitoring of progress and consolidation for future development.

The first point concerns case and targets. The case articulates the strong arguments for an appeal while more fundamentally reaffirming and even repositioning the charity. The targets are determined by the needs, the available potential and the methods used. Subtargets must permit attainment of the total requirement.

The second point concerns actual and potential sources of funds, which have a range of means, relationships and prejudices to be allowed for by the fund-raising. The sources may seek to share a charity's service and values through their support. Research based on good hypotheses will be needed to identify, evaluate and characterise sources for an appeal.

Point 3 concerns methods, strategy, organisation and resources. Techniques selected must be capable of delivering the available potential and must be sequenced so that they reinforce and do not impede each other. Methodology must be matched, segment by segment, to the sources. Time must be allowed for techniques to become productively established. Organisation, personnel and investment must be apt and sufficient for the strategy and must be sustained so that this can deliver its targeted goals.

Point 4 concerns the record and monitoring systems which allow all funding relations to be tracked, appraised and coordinated. It also argues that the future should be built into most fund-raising strategies, allowing for consolidation of relations and increasing, long-term returns.

Introduction

This section discusses a basic discipline, applicable to all forms of fund-raising, which I have called the *fund-raising cycle*.[1] It can be used as a practical tool in a number of circumstances:

- for penetrating a problem or opportunity that needs to be analysed (if my mind goes blank when faced by a question, the cycle can restore the picture and start the analysis);
- as a basis for strategic planning, whether for a complex programme aimed at many segments of support or a simple programme aimed at a few sources only – for long-term objects or for a specific short-term goal;
- as a check on progress and method for interim appraisal as a programme develops;
- to evaluate a completed programme and to point to where to go next as the cycle renews itself.

The cycle is also, evidently, a useful device for explaining how well-structured fund-raising works; but this was never its principal or most useful function. Figure 3.1 shows how it is usually illustrated.

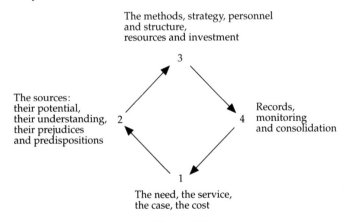

The methods, strategy, personnel and structure, resources and investment

3

The sources: their potential, their understanding, their prejudices and predispositions

2

4

Records, monitoring and consolidation

1

The need, the service, the case, the cost

Figure 3.1

The rest of this chapter discusses each of those stages in the context of a major appeal. The cycle is not a rigid mechanism. It proposes a continuous process. The case and targets generated at point 1 will be adapted, as the plan is implemented; the lists generated at point 2 by research will be revised and extended as leaders become engaged; methods determined at point 3 may be reviewed as the strategy develops; each present action will be considered for its future repercussions, anticipating point 4. There are distinct functions to be carried out and they have a logical order but there is no discontinuity between these functions.

There is also consistency with the model I proposed in the previous chapter. The cycle starts with the cause, the responsive service, the need. It next addresses the people to whom this is or could be made motivating, given their idealisms and ambitions as well as their interests and means. It considers the skills and investment required to deliver an effective programme. Finally, it considers the strengthening of relationships with people whose support has declared a sharing of hope and idealism, and has not been a cold response to a cunningly devised appeal.

Point 1: the case

The direct fund-raising purpose of the case is to establish the strong arguments giving priority to the cause, to the people or objects embraced by the need and to the responsive services which are the focus for an appeal. A much more radical purpose is a reaffirmation and possibly a repositioning of the charity: a renewal of vision and of mission. This means that, instead of defining the case simply as a well-articulated statement, an eloquent sheet of paper, it is made a function in a process of transformation. I have often seen that piece of paper suffice but new energy has flowed through the organisation and its appeal when transformation has happened.

The process of determining and committing to the case for a charity may also resist what I have described elsewhere as a law of organisational entropy, manifest in 'the demonstrable fact that political regimes and other human institutions seem to gather into themselves the causes of their own corruption and the contradiction of their inspiring idealism almost from the moment they are formed'.[2]

I start with the more radical purpose, because the process may conclude that no appeal is needed; or that the appeal must reach out to bolder objectives which more adequately match the needs than those originally proposed. Both situations arise. I had a client who, over the years, insisted that £10m was needed but could never prove this. No appeal could be justified partly because aspects of their activity appeared unnecessary and partly because they could not show why an under-used asset should not be sold, for more than £10m. More frequently, the charity has underestimated its real requirements, perhaps because it prejudged that the required targets were unattainable. The same resource may be demanded to attain either target – the one that achieves or the one that falls short of the needs.

That underrates the benefits of the process. Think of what it entails, if taken earnestly. It starts by redescribing the cause, using the best available knowledge and facts. What is its priority in the world of needs? What is its priority in people's minds? It moves on to redefine the actual and required position and roles for this agency, allowing for other agencies in or adjoining its field. Is it focused on the right needs? Should it redirect activity to achieve its objects more adequately? What is the quality of its service? Who else is operating in the same field? Do they do the same job, possibly better? What is its distinctive role? Is this of value? Or are we inadequate, redundant? What – if we have a role – would be our most adequate response to vision and mission?

An organisation can be revitalised if it goes through such a process: questioning past, present and future; constructively engaging its key people. In doing this, it may spin a web of interest and involvement around the people with whom it needs to work in its fund-raising. At the same time, it may also produce those useful pieces of paper.

The process must allow for its context. People outside the charity may have little awareness or understanding of the cause. Unless they are specialists, they will not clearly know what has been the impact of government's changed provisions for the unemployed, the poor, the disabled; or what effect government cuts have had on the agencies that should respond to those people's needs. Among the people served by these agencies there may be some, like Aids sufferers or young offenders, for whom there is too little unprompted sympathy; and others, like lone parents, against whom prejudice seems recently to have been orchestrated. There are other issues if, for example, the very different situations of two universities designated OU are to be considered: Oxford University is a world-renowned institution, a place for recognition and memorials, with many powerful alumni; the Open University is respected, has few powerful alumni, yet is one of the world's greatest innovators in higher and further education, whose founding vision came out of the future. Such factors fundamentally affect determination of a charity's case.

In developing the case, you are not simply sharpening the organisation's marketing messages or propositions. You should also, internally with staff and volunteers, be revitalising enthusiasm, commitment and ambition for service. Externally you should be affirming a new or renewed vision and mission and inviting participation in these.

All this urges people in or related to organisations to dream constructively, to project their ambitions for service boldly, without prejudging the external support that those dreams and ambitions could generate. There is the heart and centre of energy for the charity.

The targets

What follows must be a very realistic exercise, which sets funding as well as operational targets for those dreams and ambitions. This part of the cycle has to be totally realistic as well as visionary and challenging. The arguments supporting the case and targets will be critically examined by the people whose support you are seeking. They must be moved emotionally, but their judgements must also be convinced; which means that they must understand the nature and priority of the cause and also the organisation's distinctive role which, with their support, will make the difference. That means that the organisation's programme of work must be described and explained, whether this relates to a continuation and extension of established practice or to new developments. The base for the argument and for the projected targets should be the organisation's (rolling) three- or five-year plan. The process by which the funding propositions are articulated will include discussion with key staff and volunteers and scrutiny of relevant documents. Such consultations may be extended to some selected outsiders, to secure their objective view and also to initiate their involvement in the cause.

The corporate and business plans will define the organisation's competitive position and the sums needed to fulfil its mission, including developments. This is one way in which targets for fund-raising may be set. The process will be more or less exact, depending on circumstances. For a capital objective such as a building or piece of equipment, calculation of the requirement may be reasonably exact, although supporters will want to know that, when the doors open or the machine is switched on, there will be income from fees or other sources which will sustain operations for the years to come. Similarly, if there is a specific programme of work to be funded, there may be fairly exact calculation of what is needed, perhaps relating to particular salaries and overheads. A charity may need to set a complex target: for example, £x for the capital need, £y yearly for the first three years of operation, with a separate but related exercise – using membership, direct marketing, earned income and legacies – designed to secure longer-term funding.

The process is often fairly inexact. The charity may be able to spend any sums it can raise, so that there is no precise definition to the requirement. I am often asked 'How much could we raise?', the programmes that might be undertaken being determined by the answer. There may be imperfectly calculable considerations: what target would be not just realistic, but also worthy of this charity in comparison with others? What target would deliver the best result from an arbitrary opportunity, such as an anniversary or royal function? What target, given those pursued by other charities, will mark this as one of the year's major appeals in the eyes of potential supporters? As well as needing to be for important objectives, the target must also challenge and catch the imagination.

Where it cannot be calculated exactly, the target should be set high enough to realise the potential of the appeal's component units. This may relate to a particular source, a company, an individual or a trust; or it may relate to a local or regional part of the appeal – Manchester, Devon, Wales. For example, if the appeal has an open-ended target, not being based on finite needs, is it large enough to allow those local or regional units to deliver results up to their potential? Or does it ask, from Manchester or Wales, only £50,000 instead of £250,000 or more?

A point of basic importance is that prospective supporters, even when they have assented to the cause, are unlikely to know what they should give or how to do this. Of course, for some approaches the proposition will be precise: when applying for a grant from a trust for a particular purpose, when inviting somebody to endow a chair or when negotiating a sponsorship. Some sources require such specific approaches but in a large and complex appeal, while approaches should be specific about the total sums sought, they may be less precise about the objects to which a unit of support will be applied. The overall appeal must have clear objectives, covering stated causes or beneficiaries and describing the services to be delivered. These specific objects may be needed for the whole appeal in all its detail; or may make a huge target intelligible, motivating and attainable. But there can be great advantages if the bulk of funds raised is unearmarked and in fact this is how much funding in many major appeals is received, a high proportion of high-level prospects deciding on the level of support to be given rather than its precise application. Of course, the situation will vary from appeal to appeal and from source to source.

There is another way to analyse the subtargets for an appeal, which perhaps needs explanation and even defence. I have heard it criticised as too theoretical and mechanistic, by people who had not used it effectively or had yet to do so. It projects the pattern of support experienced in successful campaigns and is a valuable tool for communication on segmentation of an appeal's target and for management of an appeal's progress. For a target of £10m, the projection might be as shown in Table 3.1. The scales may vary, depending for example on actual components of the target or on the prospects available for this appeal.

Evidently, if you take out the higher sums projected, you greatly increase the number of units to be sought. The results

Table 3.1 Projection of appeal subtargets

Units of support		Scale of support
1	×	£2m
1	×	£1m
3	×	£500,000
5	×	£250,000
10	×	£100,000
25	×	£50,000
50	×	£25,000
Many smaller	×	£75,000

achieved will still taper in value from the top, as prospects with lower potential take their due rank in relation to those of higher potential. Moreover, for most appeals, there is a finite number of sources which can realistically be approached. Given that, in a successful campaign, you may need at least three times the number of prospects to the number of units projected (allowing for refusals), you may quickly multiply the units needed beyond the number of prospects available. Finally, since in a major support programme main approaches are made personally, face-to-face by committed members of the funding groups, the number of major support prospects must be limited or it will be beyond the capacity of the appeal organisation to reach them effectively.

Those are points that can be made with key appeal leaders and this is one way in which the projection can be used as a powerful fund-raising communication. Discussion of the table can set the early levels of giving which act as markers for the appeal that follows. As the appeal progresses and units change from projections to attainments, gaps in the projected pattern can indicate at what levels fund-raising activity should be concentrated. Once, highest units in an appeal clustering between £1m and £1.5m, levels had to be raised to £5m to £10m for £250m to be achieved. Elsewhere, could the result be clinched with two additional sums above £100,000? Or with ten at around £20,000? The abstract units projected may be related to particular appeal components or objectives.

I use three examples:

1. At the moment that first markers need to be set for subsequent giving, there might be a private meeting with the person chairing the appeal. The focus for discussing the first pledges of support and the implications if these are set below the required levels can be that very table. Conversation could follow some such line as this: *You will need to achieve pace-setting results at the levels projected; the first move must be made now; if this is set at the right, challenging level its consequences will be (further high level support/confidence that the targets can be achieved/an example to remoter prospects); if the markers are set too low at this point, there will be failure or an over-protracted campaign, because (there are too few prospects/ achievement must be sooner/we cannot be credible without such initiating leadership).*

2. A facility is needed for young, unmarried, pregnant women in a conservative town. The council will provide a building and there will be fees to match revenue costs but £30,000 must be found to equip the place and to give it a hopeful start. Only twenty sufficiently prosperous families are interested and motivated to support the project. Broader significant support has been tested and has failed. Therefore the message is clear, given the known unequal means but roughly equal commitment to the cause of the people identified. The communication is naturally close and personal. The proposed pattern of support, intensely discussed and approximately achieved using that table, but which delivers the required sum, is as follows:
    (a) £5,000 from one source (an architect, I think);
    (b) £3,000 from two sources (a senior civil servant and a professional);
    (c) £2,000 from six sources (various senior and middle-ranking professionals and managers);
    (d) £1,000 from ten sources (sources as above).

3. A vast new resource is wanted in a county, by industry and the local authorities. There is a target of £50m. There must be a demonstration of support from the corporate, private and statutory bodies within the county if sufficient outside support is to be secured. Ten million pounds has been allocated by the county; two other local authorities have committed £1m and £500,000. The sums needed from

companies and individuals in the area are well above anything they have given before (£25,000 is the highest figure we have heard of); and the enterprise was originated by them. There are few sources in the county. Demands must fall on them according to their means. So the messages to early prospects, including originators of the enterprise, are clear and set unprecedented challenges. Table 3.2 shows the kind of pattern of support that has to be achieved if the enterprise is to succeed, in terms of its ambition and timespan. Following discussion of this requirement, the chairman of the fund-raising group pledges £500,000 and is followed at this level by two other medium-sized companies. This puts upward pressure on the main national companies and utilities in the region. This promises the first £5m corporate funding from about eight sources and sets the pace for the programme. We predicted problems if support at this stage clustered around and below £100,000. Meanwhile, a family which did not qualify for the major prospect list pledges £50,000, setting a new high marker for a different segment of support.

It is not only the prospective sources for an appeal who need targets. Staff, volunteers and committees need them in order to raise performance and to motivate them. Such targets are also a vital aspect of appeal management.

My last point on targets is one of realism: they should be challenging and motivating. They should also comprehend an organisation's foreseeable needs, since it may not soon be able to mount another major appeal.

Table 3.2

Units of support		Scale of support
1	×	£10m
1	×	£5m
1	×	£3m
5	×	£1m
7	×	£500,000
10	×	£250,000
25	×	£100,000

This raises a different issue, which has latterly faced me more frequently. This is because over the last few years the funding requirements of some charities have taken another quantum leap. The point for fund-raising is that prospective major supporters should know the scale of the consequent demand without the overall and detailed propositions for a particular appeal losing their credibility. For the highest levels of potential supporters, it is important that they know and believe that *here* is one of the most significant objects for funding over the next ten to twenty years: significant because of its impact in a main field of concern and, perhaps, because it offers a singular opportunity to make a beneficial difference through singular wealth; for some, to earn recognition and a memorial; for others, in proportion to their generosity, to deliver one of the greatest satisfactions in a lifetime. Yet, for most causes, including ancient universities, it may be difficult to project credible funding priorities beyond, say, five years, although it is known that requirements will exceed and justify funds dimensions higher over ten to twenty years.

Therefore it is not only sensible but necessary, if the highest levels of funding are to be achieved, to use a model that projects, say, three- to five-year priority requirements for funding against, say, a ten- to twenty-year *horizon* of need, which lifts vision, ambition and opportunity to the scale of the likely total need. That can set £100 million against a £250 million horizon; £250 million against a £1 billion horizon – justifying shorter and longer targets and so releasing funds at the highest, unprecedented levels. And having set out on such a fund-raising journey in response to needs, when one horizon has been reached, another is ahead.

Point 2: the sources of funds

Whatever I have said about shared values and ideals, the test for fund-raising is to secure the funds required. People and organisations give support for reasons ranging from altruism to self-interest. I have even seen a large sum given in order to spite another donor. From a charity's point of view, the fund-raising objective is attained when over time it gets the funds it needs, provided that the sources and motives are acceptable to it. Trustees should carefully consider their responsibilities to the charity they serve before they turn support away. There will be some categories of organisation from which a charity should not accept support – alcohol and tobacco with young people's or cancer and heart disease causes, for example. The same stricture would apply to a charity's association with the promotion of a product or service. NSPCC properly refused to benefit from the *Sun*'s promotion of the 'Dianagate' tapes. And some funds are absolutely tainted. Support from sources close to Maxwell, BCCI and Polly Peck naturally caused anxieties. However, my point is positive. A successful appeal will attract support from many types of people and organisation, variously motivated. To succeed it must understand these people and their motivations. Charities would be unwise, even irresponsible, fanatically to preclude support from many large providers of support. One of those 'Years of the Whatever' bodies once told me that they would accept no funds from any company associated with the defence industry (or alcohol, tobacco, anti-trades unionism), which blocked them from electronics, construction, food, transport, engineering and almost any other category imaginable, except perhaps the wonderful Scott Bader group.[3]

My point about shared values and ideals may be viewed as one important aspect of fund-raising methodology. Few charities have their supporters' salvation as an object. People and organisations give support for many types of reason:

- Out of shared idealism, to identify with the charity and its cause, even to participate, if these are admitted and structured by the charity. Philanthropy and altruism are motives too easily discounted in fund-raising.
- For personal advantage, in terms of perceived status and acknowledgement; or for public or peer-group recognition; or for self-satisfaction.
- For corporate or product advantage, whether in terms of sales or perceptions and image.
- Out of mutual obligation in relation to someone already identified with the cause; perhaps as a result of peer example and persuasion; because of the person who asks.
- Because there is a mass movement for the cause: publicity,

everyone joining in, multiple opportunities to participate, apparent universality – increasing returns.

I do not include feelings of guilt, because they have seldom been useful to me, interesting though they are for debate. For some causes, fear may be a motive, but that is a form of self-interest.

At this second point in the cycle, the aim is to find who and where are the people and organisations with whom there is a prima-facie reason for their taking an interest; with the means to respond to an appeal at the levels required; to whom there is or could be access by the charity.

There will usually need to be research which identifies the prospects, locates them, makes an assessment of their fund-raising potential and sees what networks of contacts, if any, are available to reach them. A charity that has fund-raised in the past, has webs of contacts through its honorary committees and other structures, keeps records, has a different starting point from one that has done none of these things or which, for example, has until now used only direct marketing methods with no major support programmes. In either case similar research procedures are needed, although the plans and their implementation begin with different opportunities.

First, there need to be some good hypotheses about the people, companies and trusts who are the charity's most promising prospects. The process must start with donors, sponsors, volunteers and traders who have a demonstrated interest in supporting the charity. A charity that has such good connections and a track record can partly base its hypotheses on reflection, but should not assume that its future will mirror its past. That may give the charity that has no relevant past an advantage, though not of course in terms of contacts. The contrasts can be very marked: between Oxford or Cambridge University, whose distinguished and rich alumni fill tomes, and the Open University, with a great reputation and few powerful friends; between the Royal Academy of Arts, with its attractive networks for contacts, and the Northern Ireland Voluntary Trust, dealing in a field unpopular for fund-raising and which, when it was a new body, had no records or contact networks; between NSPCC, a charity with a popular cause and strong contacts unen-cumbered by ideological restrictions in fund-raising, and Shelter, which might be perceived as non-establishment, dealing with a vital but tough cause, where staff questioned whether there were rich individuals and powerful business leaders who could share the charity's idealism.

Those hypotheses, which will give initial direction to the research, must consider likely awareness, prejudices, attitudes and motives. These may need to be tested. The kinds of assumption have been that NSPCC could direct a concerted appeal at the whole conscious population; that the Northern Ireland Voluntary Trust should start by looking at London-based individuals (because that was where major funding decisions were made) with roots in Northern Ireland; that there were rich and powerful people who would support Shelter and share its idealism – but that staff would have to be persuaded of this before major support fund-raising began; that CAFOD should concentrate on professionals such as doctors and lawyers, where Roman Catholics were relatively highly represented, while the few rich Catholic individuals could be dealt with separately. The hypotheses will take account of the type and context of the particular appeal. It may be relevant to very few prospects. It may be launched at a time when two or more major appeals run in its sector; when there is acute competition for sources and for leadership. It may have national, regional, local or international scope – or all of these.

The research undertaken should reflect the charity's situation today and its fund-raising purpose (see Figure 3.2). Research based on this model must have the future as its focus because it is not an exercise in history. It is part of a dynamic, progressive process. The research undertaken may serve any of a number of purposes, from broad advertising to segmented direct marketing to major support programmes. Its purposes for the latter may also vary: mapping networks for access to sources, identifying leaders or giving detailed information before briefings to individuals and organisations.

The types of source of primary concern here are non-statutory. National and local government, the EU and international funding agencies are all important for project, core and challenge funding but they need separate treatment. I am mainly concerned with individuals, trusts and companies. From my major-support viewpoint, associations of individuals or

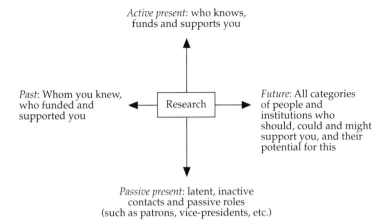

Active present: who knows,
funds and supports you

Past: Whom you knew,
who funded and
supported you

Research

Future: All categories
of people and
institutions who
should, could and might
support you, and their
potential for this

Passive present: latent, inactive
contacts and passive roles
(such as patrons, vice-presidents, etc.)

Figure 3.2

companies (like Lions or Round Table) can dissipate funding persuasion and reduce the unit and aggregate sums achieved.

Immediately, a new point must be made. The focus must be on the people who make the decisions where gifts, grants, sponsorships, promotions and employee support go. This should dissolve some internal barriers that charities set up for the organisation of fund-raising and research. Private individuals make their own decisions as to where they give support to charities. Most rich individuals and families use trusts or foundations, which are interchangeable terms, as their vehicles for giving support. Those vehicles may have policies and some will have directors but in most cases it is an individual or a family member who decides whether major support will be given to *this* or *that* cause. The professional directors, whom I have described as chauffeurs as distinct from owner-drivers, will protest at this because it detracts from their status. They are of course important and must be cultivated; but there may be fewer than ten major trusts in the United Kingdom where a rich individual or family does not make many of the crucial decisions on major support, of course using their employed advisers and administrators.

It may seem surprising to people little engaged in major support fund-raising that the same principle applies to most companies, even where there are a public affairs or donations committee and a policy on support for voluntary causes. In most reasonably large companies there will be a number of routes through which support can be given, entailing various entry points to the company. Thus there may be: a donations budget and procedure; promotions and sponsorship policies, focused on marketing people and their budgets; an employee support policy, perhaps focused on the personnel department. There may even be environmental, educational, European affairs and other policies, with related budgets and personnel. A charity may have the programme that matches the criteria for support from one of these divisions in which case, provided this will not prevent some more productive intended approach, a proposition should probably be made at its ordained place within the company. However, if, for example, it has been decided that this company should within the universe of prospects be targeted for, say, £1m, a sum beyond the capacity of any one budget, then there must be a different approach. It is usually difficult to upgrade the level of contact and support from a single budget-holder within a company. We were recently asked by one such to go to the chairman, because only in this way could support, which he wanted to provide, be given on the scale needed. If the contact and main persuasion are with the senior decision-maker in a company – who perhaps also holds a controlling interest in it – first, there can be a commitment to the sum targeted; then, if necessary, there can be an allocation of subtargets within the company, so that the figure required can for example be achieved through collaboration between family trust, board, marketing and employees.

For many of these funding decisions the person to be identified may be privately rich, a major shareholder and influential board member, the crucial trustee. Fund-raising should not split that funding personality. This happens when a charity's fund-raising and research are rigidly compartmentalised. It is the person who makes the decisions who has to be identified and involved for fund-raising. That has implications for the fund-raising and for the research.

These points determine where the research should concentrate and how it should proceed. It must identify the decision-makers but also describe the policies, gross incomes, fund-dispensing systems, previous grants, sponsorship and promotional budgets of the companies and trusts identified. These facts about previous performance should not determine the types and levels of proposition made. Good fund-raising changes such realities, where it can. It subverts the systems. The research should also show what previous support, if any, the charity has received from the prospects being researched and with whom contacts were made. The detail on people, as individuals in their trust or corporate roles, needs to include a range of factors if structured contacts and relations are to be established with them. Beyond basic details of name, age, occupation and status, data can include school, college, regiment, religion, board and trust membership and clubs, interests on any one or combination of which a successful contact and approach may depend.

This phase of research has these aspects:

- A review and audit of records.
- Desk research using the standard directories and guides.
- A constant survey of newspapers and journals.

The products of that phase of research will be lists and profiles of prospects, with a map of the charity's networks for contacts with them if such exist. These first lists will be prefigurements of future relations, including phantom names as yet without substance for this charity. The names begin to become real, the prospects to have substance as the draft lists are discussed within the charity's first networks and then with its extending range of contacts. The lists become active when those contacts enliven them through their involvement and advocacy for the charity and cause.

This suggests that there must be speed and flexibility in the computerised systems through which the information is stored, collated, accessed and disseminated. Is it possible to inter-connect active contacts and prospects across the factors used in the system? Can the system track the history of each relationship, in terms of positive and negative outcomes and contacts? Within a large organisation, can it inform different sectors of who is handling or has handled each contact, so that there can be coordination and control and so that it is known who is doing what to and with whom? Does the system allow for analysis and segmentation of prospects and of supporters?

That description by no means covers the range of research a charity may undertake. Many will want to take a quantitative measure of levels of support across and within segments of the community, measuring its position absolutely in terms of performance and relatively in relation to the competition. It could choose to do this at any time; but particularly before, during and after an intense, concerted campaign through which awareness, attitudes and performance were to be shifted. For this a special survey may be commissioned or some questions might be inserted into an established omnibus survey. Equally, a charity may want to take a qualitative look at attitudes, prejudices and levels of understanding and awareness in relation to the cause served, the charity and the competition. It may want to test responses to messages about itself and probe reactions. This can be done through groups or through in-depth interviews. A charity may want a lifestyle survey to describe its supporters and users, segment by segment. Indeed, a charity may want to use a combination of these, supplementing the prospect research that I have been describing. The object is clear: to know and understand the people who do or could support you, so that you can, to mutual reward, come closer to each other.

Point 3: methods, strategy, resources

A sound fund-raising strategy selects the segments of its target universe that are potentially most productive; deploys against each target segment the methods likely to achieve the fullest attainable realisation of potential; and orders those methods so that, at best, they reinforce each other and, at least, they do not diminish what they yield or prevent them from yielding anything. This means that decisions are made on the people and organisations to be approached, selected according to criteria discussed in the previous section; and on the methods to be used for securing their support. What criteria are there for the selection of fund-raising methods?

Methods as well as sources have a potential yield which can be crudely estimated, provided that decisions have been reached on overall and unit targets for fund-raising. This, for example, is a comparative illustration, which I have called a ladder of effectiveness.

1.	Individual to peer with close acquaintance or friendship, the approach being made person-to-person by somebody financially committed at the appropriate level.	10
2.	Committed individual to peer group, as above, with personal written or telephoned follow-up.	8
3.	Other approaches peer-to-peer, person-to-person as above but without prior personal acquaintance.	6
4.	As in 1, but by letter.	5
5.	Individual to peer group as in 2, without personal acquaintance but with personal follow-up.	5
6.	General, personalised mailing from somebody known to and respected by recipients but not acquainted with them.	4
7.	General, non-personalised mailing.	3
8.	Leaflet drop with personal, non-peer visit.	2
9.	Leaflet drop without personal visit.	1
10.	Response to editorial.	1
11.	Response to advertising.	0.5
12.	Any of the above badly executed.	−10

Note: This is a fallible model. Editorial and advertising have important roles supporting other forms of fund-raising and marketing; either can deliver large units of support, but neither would be a sound choice for securing many such units and for sustaining such support over time.

A prospect may be exposed to more than one kind of method, provided that this does not depress performance. For example, a £100,000 supporter might be involved in certain events but would probably be spared the direct mail solicitation for £250. My qualification is that, within an intense funding programme, the stronger proposition should generally be made first, the weaker later, to provide *multiple, progressive and cumulative opportunities for giving*. An actual example from the same source over a year is as follows:

£100,000 gift → £25,000 to attend exclusive dinner → £5,000 for
two seats at gala opera performance

In this instance, the £100,000 would not have been achieved if the £25,000 had come first. This does not mean that a £50,000 pledge cannot be converted to £100,000. I have seen refusals converted to £500,000. Such progressions may be achieved but are exceptional.

The importance of a related point has been impressed on me by experience in three major programmes over the last few years. Fund-raising is a form of marketing, although its values and the relationships it fosters go beyond anything achieved by ordinary product or corporate marketing. This is why people with marketing skills can do well in fund-raising but can fail to realise potential unless they deepen their understanding. There are points about supporters' motivations and relationships with a charity and perhaps most acutely about the roles of leadership in major support programmes that require more than ordinary marketing insight. For example, many charities can make strong sponsorship, joint promotion or other propositions which may be negotiated through a company's marketing department on their intrinsic merits. That is true of a charity with or without influential fund-raising leadership. But these are not the only or necessarily the strongest methods of approach to be used and there is a limit to the number that can be made. Yet I have seen appeals in which it was decided 'to take a different approach' and to use only the marketing-type proposition. I think the charities saw this as a pioneering tactic! This removed the tough task of enlisting and mobilising fund-raising leadership. It was based on a fallacy. Indeed, in two instances, the dangerous and silly phrase 'The age of philanthropy is dead' was intoned as the resultant unsuccessful strategy was launched. One of these scattered 'salesmen' around companies, peddling propositions untainted by altruism. The salesmen delivered dismal results. Only where the abundantly available leadership was used did that appeal achieve satisfactory results from these sources. A successful fund-raising strategy which includes a major support element is able to include a component that is based on the unadorned marketing proposition and approach but is likely to fall short of potential unless it also harnesses fund-raising leadership. My point is that it should include both. They are complementary factors, not alternatives. This may be made clearer by a typical analysis of a prospect universe by segments for a broad fund-raising strategy: see, for example, Table 3.3.

Where relevant, government, local authority, EU and overseas funding would be added. The table is meant to be illustrative, not exhaustive. Note that, to achieve some required target, a source may combine a number of different forms of support: trust and board grant, sponsorship, promotion, employee fund-raising, possibly with a challenge to employees.

Matters cryptically alluded to in that table, such as 'leadership', 'specific proposition' and 'high-target mailings' are dealt with later. The point here is that there must be a rigorous strategy to order and manage such a complex mixture of target groups and methods. Principles mentioned above were that methods should reinforce, not clash with, each other and that prospects should usually be exposed to stronger methods and higher propositions before receiving weaker, lower ones. With most charities this creates a problem during the period leading up to a major support programme and into its opening phase. The charity must continue to generate income. This may well include contacts with some companies, trusts and rich individuals who would be prospects for major support, well above their present levels. The problem cannot be ignored. It causes no difficulty if, for example, the sources concerned already give at high levels, since they can become part of the programme's early leadership, with no immediate request for additional support. Nor will there necessarily be difficulty where, for example, a strong sponsorship or promotional proposition is being negotiated at marketing level within a company. The problem arises with rich individuals, major

Table 3.3

Type of source	Methods of approach	Forms of support
Rich individuals	Personal contact Peer persuasion Specific propositions Exclusive dinners, functions Major, gala events Mop-up: high-target mailing	Gifts, grants Often through trusts Sponsorships Leadership Payments for events, materials Legacies
Prosperous individuals	Where possible, personal contact Peer groups with mail follow-up High-target mailings Events and functions Trading	Gifts Group funding, sponsorships Subscriptions Payments for events, materials Leadership Legacies
Major companies	Personal, peer contact with chairman, chief executive Back-up at management level Contact only at management level Specific propositions Exclusive functions Mop-up: mailed propositions Sometimes through agencies	Gifts, grants Sponsorships Promotions Employee fund-raising Leadership (Corporate membership) Payments for events, materials
Medium-sized companies	Where possible, chairman contact Management-level contacts Group presentations Mailed propositions Events, functions Maybe local, regional	Gifts, grants Sponsorships Promotions Corporate memberships Perhaps employees Local leadership Payments for events, materials
Major trusts	Peer contact with trustee(s) Senior staff contact with directors Group briefings for trustees, directors Specific propositions Mop-up: mailed specific propositions	Grants Sustained support
Other trusts	Letters and telephone Specific propositions Local, regional contacts and briefings	Grants Sustained support
General public	Direct marketing Supporter group House-to-house Events, functions Trading Through Lions, Round Table, schools, charities, street collections	Gifts Memberships Subscriptions Payments Volunteering Legacies

companies and trusts who must give high levels of support within the appeal but who are now targeted, not perhaps for fairly harmless sums like £5, £50 or £100, but for low multiples of £1,000 which, when given and acknowledged, could satisfy them as their support for this cause. It will be very difficult soon to return to such supporters with a higher, more appropriate proposition. For example, a prospect being cultivated for £1m nationally receives a request for £25,000 from international headquarters which, if given, exempts them from all future fund-raising. Exasperated by such a double approach, the source shifts support elsewhere. Result: £1,025,000 lost. Or the prospect may give the £25,000 and accept the exemption and the glory. Result: £975,000 lost. There needs to be negotiation on the charity's golden list of main prospects. There must also be realism, balancing this year's £1,000 against next year's possible £100,000 or some greater sum but recognising that this year's income must meet this year's needs.

The strategy must not allow the triggering of responses from prospects well below their potential. On the other hand, it must allow different methods to reinforce each other, so that the total appeal builds its own energy, momentum and coherence. For example, a public relations campaign can attract the kind of uncontrolled premature response that is to be avoided; or it can raise awareness and strengthen messages at moments of advantage. An event wrongly timed, aimed at the major support universe and with a high entry cost, can confuse the message and dissipate support; or, aptly timed, it may be the celebration rounding off the appeal, giving major supporters an additional opportunity to contribute, reinforcing relations for the future. Aptly planned public relations, delivering recognition of the person, the company or the product, these having been pre-arranged and even contracted, can clinch or be a crucial factor in a source's commitment of support.

One implication is that the strategic timetable must allow time to build the programme strongly. If there is a major support element, which requires there to be one or more bodies of powerful leaders who will take responsibility for raising subtargets within the total requirement, there must be time to enlist, inform and motivate them and to secure their support at exemplary levels. I discuss this later, noting here three common impulses of directors, trustees and senior management which can destroy a nascent funding programme. First, there is insistence on an early 'launch' – whatever that means. I believe that, if 'launches' there must be, there may need to be more than one. For example, in a major support programme, the enlistment of leadership may start with a private 'launch'; the major support element itself would be 'launched' to the balance of prospects only when 30–50 per cent of the target had been pledged and there was a sufficient body of qualified leaders to follow up the launch; the public 'launch' might be of a different kind, aimed at the general public and giving publicity to the charity and the cause it served. Indeed, every group briefing may be regarded as a 'launch' to that segment of the target universe. In many appeals, there should be national, regional and local 'launches'.

Another impulse is to rush the appointment of a chairperson, which may lumber the appeal with an unqualified leader; or one with too little authority; or one with authority but too few contacts; or one who will not give the time needed or use his or her contacts; or one who is indifferent to the cause and perhaps disagrees with the appeal's methodology. Any one of these can devastate the programme or leave it in sloth or disarray.

Finally, there is expectation by trustees, staff and colleagues of early results, putting pressure on fund-raising staff and volunteers to rush the process and make premature approaches for funds. The outcome is likely to be underattainment.

The kind of timetable needed for a fairly simple appeal might look like Figure 3.3.

The actual timetable can be far more complex than this. There may be regional and local elements to be added. NSPCC's strategy included the creation of sixty new local fund-raising groups, in parallel with its established regional organisation. There may also need to be a programme aimed at the 'prosperous' category proposed in Table 3.3. Further, as will be discussed in the next section, even during the appeal's active phase, procedures and measures for its consolidation must be designed and introduced. At all points, there will be a need for communications aids. The point of Figure 3.3 is to give an optimistic impression of likely timescales. Each short heading in the table embraces a number of activities. For example:

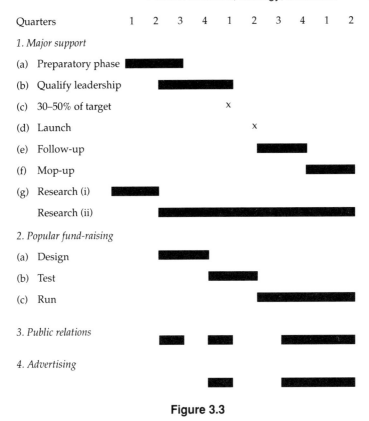

Figure 3.3

1(a) *Preparatory phase*: Establish case and targets; draft brief on these; consultations inside and outside the organisation; form steering group, including some possible leaders or people who can reach and influence candidates for leadership; prepare draft fund-raising prospectus.

1(b) *Qualify leadership*: Enlist fund-raising leaders; create nucleus for one or more fund-raising groups; secure (conditional) pledges from leaders at exemplary levels; perhaps secure a few pledges from other sources.

1(c) *30–50% of target*: These sums having been pledged from early leaders and some other close sources, prepare promotional materials for concluding period of fund-raising; brief leaders for launch and follow-up.

1(d) *Launch*: Focused on the balance of major support prospects.

1(e) *Follow-up*: By leaders, staff and other key volunteers within a few weeks of the launch; what is achieved here is what many trustees expect to be achieved within weeks of hiring the charity's fund-raising executive.

1(f) *Mop–up*: Through personal contact if this is still possible, but mostly through high-targeted mailings; to the balance of major support prospects.

1(g) *Research (i)*: An audit of records and research into existing contacts and people with strong prima-facie reasons for paying attention; to identify and list early prospective leaders.

Research (ii): Continuing research into prospects; extending maps of networks for contacts; profiling crucial prospective sources; creating living lists through actual contacts and fund-raising; remaining vigilant for opportunities, for example by scanning the press and through private enquiry.

2. *Popular fund-raising*: Using a range of techniques (including those proposed in Table 3.3); probably extending well beyond the period suggested in the timetable.

3. *Public relations*: For example, without soliciting funds, to raise awareness of the issues and of the charity, to give strong messages which would encourage recruitment; to support the launch and begin announcement of success; to support popular fund-raising; to give acknowledgement and to meet the requirements of some major supporters.

4. *Advertising*: If used, perhaps to increase numbers of regular supporters; to create interest and awareness at times of intense popular fund-raising; as part of a joint product promotion.

Having made much of targeting, planning and organisation, I finish this section by stressing that precise outcomes may not in all cases be foreseeable. Thus the strategy may have projected top levels of support at, say, £10,000, £500,000 or even £10m. The structures may be designed for this. Research may have proposed prospects who could deliver such sums. Without such preparation the required result may be unlikely. Yet the support, when it comes, may be from an unexpected source or direction: in my experience, £10,000 from somebody off the main prospect list who had just inherited, setting the first marker in a £100,000 campaign; £500,000 from a Japanese tycoon; £8m from a newly successful businessman identified as the programme developed. Sound and thorough groundwork create the possibility for such achievement.

Investment and resources

Given the scale and complexity of what may be entailed, the means must be provided to deliver the results targeted. That obvious point is often missed by trustees and by senior charity management, especially where these people are inexperienced in fund-raising. There are two typical situations: where insufficiently skilled staff are employed (because, after all, the situation is clear, and requires no over-priced genius to resolve it); or where staff, skilled or unskilled, are employed, then refused the budgets and resources that would allow them to succeed (because, if they know their job, they should get on with it). There is an even more insidious form of the same disease where the right staff and resources are deployed but senior trustee and management support are qualified or withheld, presumably because they do not believe in the strategy – they will be blameless if it fails, and will preen themselves if it succeeds. This casts fund-raising as a detached, self-sufficient, quasi-magical role which functions independently of the cause and of the quality and value of the charity's services.

There can be no promise or expectation of rapid returns. Reciprocally, an appeal whose preliminaries become interminable, because there are real difficulties or because fund-raisers and charity dither and lack credibility, dissipates energy and loses hope.

A practical issue emerging from this relates to investment. If I say that total costs for a major appeal (covering salaries, other internal overheads, materials, external services and all other items) may total 10 per cent of the target to be raised and that 25 per cent of those costs may need to be spent before returns are seen, this shows the measure of nerve, courage and foresight required of a charity's decision-makers.

What are the requirements?

- A determined initial budget commitment which relates to realistic objectives for performance.
- Regular review, so that actual achievement in relation to expenditure may be understood and evaluated.
- Sustained moral and financial support, unless the indicators are negative. Staff and volunteers become demoralised if they feel, whatever the success or failure, that they must repeatedly justify themselves to hostile tribunals within the charity.

Of course, patently unproductive investment will be cut off but productivity should be assessed within the agreed strategic timescale. There can be a crisis, even in a programme running to schedule, at the point of maximum expenditure before significant returns are seen. Yet this is the point at which the game is lost or won. An old friend once said at this point: 'Redmond, if I come away from the company today with only £100, I'll feel my job is justified.' At a crucial moment, he was under pressure and doubted his own effectiveness. A few months later that company delivered £100,000.

Figure 3.4 shows a graph, based roughly on a real situation, which illustrates this point. The graph reflects returns on investment for a particular appeal, not returns on total investment for the charity over ten years. The investment principle implied in the graph does, I claim, apply to any fund-raising method and would be more precisely measurable for, say, a direct marketing exercise. There will usually be maximum outlay on a method just before returns are seen. In a major support programme this is the moment when staff, materials and functions are funded and poised to function. The case that this table reflects is a complex programme over a few years. As with a company launching a new product, risks were entailed.

The curve represents net return on investment. It is impressionistic, not statistically accurate. The *homunculus* reflects trustees' and senior management's attitudes at different moments. In this case the periods are years. The investment figures were cumulative: £1.5 million was the approximate total

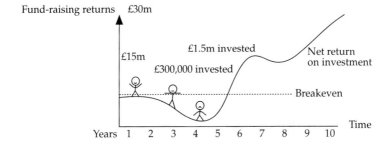

Figure 3.4

cost. Because the people, skills, structures and procedures were kept in place after the intense appeal, income continued to soar after an initial drop when publicity and popular participation declined and there was some exhaustion among staff and volunteers. During the recession, income fell back again but remained at vastly enhanced levels compared to year 1.

The complex action discussed here requires organisational structures and procedures which allow direction, coordination, oversight and management to work. The design of such structures and procedures would be part of the strategy. Points in the cycle interact and overlap which is why, for convenience, I leave these matters to the next section. For a charity whose interests are in a long-term programme rather than a one-off appeal, those structures and procedures are parts of its investment in the future, as should have been demonstrated.

Point 4: consolidation

For any charity whose funding requirements will continue and grow for the future, the introduction of new methods, skills and above all relationships should not be for a brief period only, unless they have proved unproductive. Only bits of what I have to say in this section are relevant to a campaign with one-off fund-raising goals: for example, the funding of a building or piece of equipment where operating incomes are secure from elsewhere. For almost all other charity fund-raising, appeal-by-appeal, year-by-year fund-raising is a developing function. Hence my use of the cycle to analyse and order that process. To put this another way, a charity that fails to consolidate gains from an intense funding exercise is failing to realise its investment and potential.

A charity that designs its consolidation programmes properly should benefit from increasing gains, as is illustrated in the example in Figure 3.4. The structures for an intense major support programme may provide vehicles for consolidation at its term, if they are preserved. During such an intense programme, the charity will have harnessed a number of powerful people to its fund-raising, including some of the busiest and most influential people in the nation, region or community concerned. Their functions within the intense programme will be finite, in terms of time, meetings and the number of contacts to be made by them. A few of these leaders will have been particularly effective. In any such group I expect a third to be excellent, a third to be ordinary but lifted by those who are excellent, and a third to be ineffectual. Some of the excellent third will have come close to the cause and the charity and will want to continue association with them. These will be people accustomed to authority, with an interest in the cause and this charity's response to needs within it; but they will not themselves be specialists, as the charity's trustees and staff may be, in responsive service. Nor would they generally want to be concerned with the charity's routine housekeeping and management. Their skills are different and may most usefully be harnessed to the charity's funding development.

A strong model for consolidating such relationships, to be introduced as the organisational structure for the intense phase of the programme, could look like Figure 3.5.

The foundation (or whatever else it may be called) would normally be chaired by a powerful, financially committed outside supporter of the charity. Other members would be similarly qualified. The charity would have a specified number or proportion of *ex officio* and nominated members on the foundation, and the foundation would be represented on the charity board. The foundation would be bound to support objects and policies as defined by the charity board at any time. Membership of the foundation would be for a predetermined

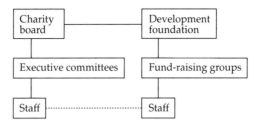

Figure 3.5

period: say, not more than two consecutive three-year terms. This can prevent ossification and make it easier to shed members no longer useful to the group. The model may be adapted. Staffing might be by the charity although, if development staff are put directly under the foundation, this takes them out of the charity's pay structures and puts budgetary responsibility with the foundation's trustees.

That model is comfortable and familiar for most fund-raising leaders, giving them due status and authority. It assumes the creation of a separate but related trust alongside the charity. It is a model that has worked with charities of all kinds where it has been used appropriately: arts organisations, universities, and welfare and health bodies. It offers distinctive opportunities for harnessing special people to the charity's fund-raising. Yet it can be seen as threatening by charity trustees, perhaps compromising their integrity. They may fear such powerful people neighbouring them. There have been bad experiences with such funding bodies but the safeguards built into my description should reduce the risks and fears.

A weaker model looks like Figure 3.6.

This structure gives weaker status and authority to the people involved and may be less satisfactory to them. Otherwise, qualifications for membership of the board (or whatever else it is called) are the same as for the foundation. Such weaker models can work but are more difficult to sustain.

That is not the only level at which consolidation is needed or the sole method for achieving it. A complex strategy deploys a variety of communications and marketing techniques. With all techniques, where the return to the charity's service merits this,

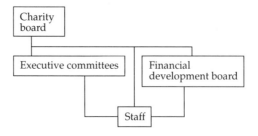

Figure 3.6

my old tag applies: 'Through marketing to relationships beyond marketing; you become part of their lives.' Methods to be used will vary from charity to charity. They start with acknowledgement, perhaps also with recognition and sustained status; they continue through regular information and contact; they flourish more with donor receptions and field visits; they may extend beyond this to regular personal contacts where, at a level of support below major but above ordinary, there is an assigned 'account handler'; and they may culminate in personal activity and involvement. One illustration of an ideal is where a main benefactor flies to visit the charity, meets its director who mentions on the tour that £50,000 will complete the project, and is given the cheque – a procedure and relationship which continue. There is an even better situation where the benefactor who has secured several hundreds of thousands of pounds from his family trusts for the costs of a bold programme sits on the steering group which will initiate its funding strategy. Those relationships go well beyond mere 'marketing'.

The elementary procedures for such consolidation should be designed as part of the original strategy. For example, a model for recognition and involvement can look like Figure 3.7. Note that I assume there can be upward mobility between some categories, actively encouraged at tactically advantageous points: regular supporter to friend or member, for example; high-level supporter to committee member or patron; committee member to trustee. Presidency and some other roles will be outside structures and expectations for routine promotion within this system. Each position in the scale should carry responsibilities as well as honours.

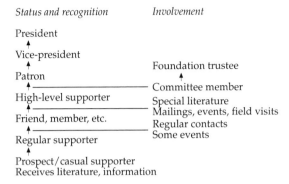

Status and recognition   *Involvement*

Figure 3.7

Consolidation extends to national and local volunteers outside the major support category. Their contribution must be credited and acknowledged, even where attribution is complicated. My view is that achievement can be attributed to more than one person or group, provided that the money is counted once only. A judgement needs to be made at the end of any intense programme using volunteers as to whether and how their involvement might be continued.

With all these measures there are mutual rewards for the supporter and the charity but the investment in consolidation must show significant returns in the service of needs, now or for the future.

To repeat my point on shared values in a different way, Figure 3.8 shows three possible modes of relationship, A being the charity, B the supporter.

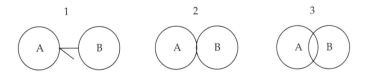

Figure 3.8

Mode 1 is a casual gesture of support, like money put into a collecting box or the purchase of a raffle ticket.

Mode 2 represents contiguity but no overlap – where there is perhaps regular or temporarily significant support with no shared values: as with a National Trust subscription if the supporter's interest is strictly in readiness and economy of access; or with attendance as a guest at a charity ball.

Mode 3 is where some involvement and relationship has been established. If the relationship were severed, there would be loss to the supporter, albeit intangible at first. The relationship is important to recipient and donor. There are shared ideals and values. The coincidence of interests, values and activities can increase. It can reach a stage at which the relationship becomes a high priority in the supporter's life, behind family and job and faith.

Each of these modes of relationship has value. In its consolidation policy the charity must decide what are the costs and benefits in upgrading such relationships.

My discussion of consolidation has several implications for staff and management. The intense programme probably increased internal skills and introduced new ones. Where these were productive, it would be unwise to lose them. The consolidation procedure I have sketched may demand new skills. Nor will the charity stand still. It will probably need to change and add to its range of techniques over any significant period. There are two conclusions for management:

- That the continuing motivation and development of staff is an essential responsibility.
- That there must be realistic, sustained development.

During the kind of programme I discussed above, computerised database and record systems would be introduced to allow for coordination and management of approaches to track the history of relationships within the programme and to allow for constant monitoring of performance. The systems would have to be flexible and accessible, to allow for constant updating of records. These systems and the information they handle must be improved (in due course replaced) and updated as an aspect of consolidation activity, which will founder without it. Even the computer programs for a charity's fund-raising development must embody its dynamism, its focus on the future rather than the past.

Key points

- Use the fund-raising cycle as a flexible tool and discipline.
- In developing the case, make the strong arguments for your cause and programme; but allow the same process to achieve a reaffirmation of objects and ideals. Targets must be set in relation to the funding requirement and the available funding potential.
- You must identify, evaluate and understand the sources for any appeal, using skilled research to do this. But another object must be to see how funding support can become a sharing of values and service.
- Fund-raising methods that are capable of realising the potential available must be used; ordered so that they reinforce each other; allowing time for them to establish themselves effectively.
- The resources, organisation and investment in an appeal must be proportionate to the methods and must be sustained so that these can deliver the results required.
- There must be monitoring and record systems which permit management and coordination of the programmes and prepare for future development.
- The strategy should almost always have built into it structures and procedures that permit long-term development of relations and of fund-raising.

4 Fund-raising leadership and process

Chapter summary

Major support fund-raising is built on personal, peer approaches. This entails the concept of leadership. Fund-raising leaders are people appropriately financially committed to an appeal who are prepared to use their contacts and personal influence to secure high levels of support from other prospective supporters. Unless the task can be completed by a single person, one or more leadership groups will be needed to take responsibility for all or part of the appeal target. To achieve synergy, mutual support and peer pressure these groups must meet and act in concert, not work in isolation or, worse, simply give their names. Where several fund-raising groups operate within an appeal, there may need to be an umbrella committee which allows for their productive interaction, coordinates their activity and prepares for consolidation after the current appeal is over. All of these groups will need to use a variety of communications with a range of aims and publics. These communications must be delivered with appropriate skills and must be designed for their disparate target publics. This must allow for the main stages in the communications process: sensual, rational and voluntary, leading to the decision and action proposed.

Fund-raising leadership

Fund-raising leadership is a matter of common sense. It has been a feature of major support fund-raising for at least two thousand years in the West and is not likely soon to become extinct.

What is a 'fund-raising leader'? It is a person who believes in the cause and who is convinced by this charity's response to the needs but who has gone two moves further, making a financial contribution high in relation to the target – providing a marker for the support to follow – and being willing personally to persuade some additional individuals and organisations to commit support at an adequately high level towards the target. Such a person must have the contacts and the persuasiveness required. A few such people will go further. They will recruit and head a qualified group of leaders or take on a group at least partly formed, which accepts joint responsibility for securing all or a proportion of the target, for example across all sectors or within a corporate sector or region or within a shared social network. A few leaders may, through the process, come even closer to the cause and charity, wanting to continue not just association but also active involvement after an intense funding programme has been completed.

Already two principles are assumed: that, to secure major support, a personal approach is needed in most cases; and that it will usually be an advantage if such fund-raising operates through active groups, task forces and committees which meet and cooperate rather than having leaders who act individually, in isolation or, far worse, simply permitting use of their names, while opening a few doors for staff to enter. I deal with the latter point first. With few exceptions, individuals operating on their own will fairly quickly exhaust their motivation and will, so that contacts are dealt with cursorily and the pace of contacts slows. Indeed, they may quite quickly run out of good contacts. Where I have seen fund-raising groups operating effectively, they have set the pace needed for contacts, with impetus from regular meetings and with encouragement as group results consolidate. There can be mutual help with difficult cases and even, where needed, transfer of contacts from one group member to another. Such groups can break up the total universe into manageable bits, agreed by members. They offer a field where peer group pressure can operate, between people who are the busiest and most powerful in the community, the nation or the world.

The first of these principles has been discussed earlier but I return to it here. The task of fund-raising leaders, once they have qualified themselves financially, is to make personal approaches to key private or institutional decision-makers for support of whatever kind to the charity concerned. Prospects will be selected for approach on the basis of a leader's readiness of access to them. These statements need some qualification. There are some sources whose constitutions or policies preclude such personal approaches; but beware of believing this too easily since such policies and declarations of policy often deceive. Occasionally there will be a fund-raising leader who is not and cannot be significantly financially committed to a cause yet who is its most effective advocate, with some or even a majority of prospects. Some appeals may be totally carried by such a person but, before deciding such a course, check thoroughly that it will not omit productive contacts with some vital sources. Mixed methods can be part of the strategy. In any case, eloquent staff or volunteer spokespeople for the charity and cause often need to accompany a fund-raising leader's approach.

That is all somewhat abstract. The examples from major support programmes occur everywhere. At village level, where I live there is someone who is a great backer and promoter of community causes, with targets in the £100,000 – £200,000 range. There are other causes on a similar scale. He is known to back his own causes substantially. He also backs those of others. Therefore, when he approaches someone known to be relatively prosperous, he has great authority to do so, especially when he has just supported their personal cause. Incidentally, this is the kind of situation in which that notorious projection of required unit gifts (see Table 3.1) can be used with simple effectiveness. If the facility is wanted, and if there are few outside sources, then the people with means must respond at the levels projected or they will not achieve what they want. Currently I am dealing with a regional programme elsewhere where this logic obtains: unless the few leading employers commit funds at levels unprecedented for them there will be insufficient reason for external sources to provide the additional millions needed.

Next, I take a fund-raising committee whose members must deliver sums between, say, £100,000 and £1 million. In normal circumstances, other members of that group will have little reason to respond at the levels required unless the chairperson has made a commitment at his or her appropriate level, which should preferably be one of the highest units, between, say, £750,000 and £1 million – whether his or her support is outright or through a mixture of methods. Indeed, unless the chairperson is so committed, he or she will depress the levels at which other group members give and may actually encourage inadequate support. In the instance of which I am thinking, the £800,000 delivered came not from the appeal chairman's own means but from the trust and board, a promotion and employees' giving from the company of which he was a director. This was sufficient to set levels for other committee members' support and for the sums they solicited elsewhere.

Events may work out less neatly, as when a chairman decided to give £75,000 when more was needed, but was then approached by two committee members who said they were prepared to give £150,000 each but would not give more than the chairman. I have recently had a regional chairman, pledged to give £500,000, who went back to a neighbouring company which had pledged £150,000 where £250,000 was needed. He got the extra £100,000, because he had authority to do this. Elsewhere, at the first meeting, one member of the committee remarked: 'I hope we all understand that it costs at least £250,000 to sit at this table!' An excellent pair of examples comes from one of the United Kingdom's great philanthropists. On one consolidation committee (a year or two after the intense programme), she said she did not want to get involved in fund-raising again, but would give £500,000, and believed that the target could largely be achieved by the people at that table. On another occasion she said she would give £1 million if the charity found nine others to do likewise. She, or rather the causes, succeeded on both occasions.

The point was strongly made at the Institute of Charity Fundraising Managers' 1991 Convention by Sir Mark Weinberg, an active private, corporate and trust philanthropist:

Even in the very biggest companies – even there you'd be wrong to think that the belief and commitment of a very small number of individuals is not still a very important factor . . . What really matters . . . is to identify the individual or individuals who are likely to be able to influence the company . . . The only reason why I want to know about which the motivations are of a particular individual is because if I know that or can guess it I know which button to try to press to get them to support a particular charity; Rule number one of charitable activity: it's who asks that often matters!

Sir Mark stressed the need to meet on a one-to-one basis.[1]

Recruitment of fund-raising leaders

Few charities have the right person or people in place, qualified and willing, as preparations begin for a strategy which includes a major support element: in other words, people with an apt financial commitment who will take some responsibility for the appeal. Most have people who can give access to potential leaders or who can engineer access to people who can give such access. Occasionally a charity has nobody of this kind. It is disastrous to start with the wrong leaders, so time must be allowed for finding them.

Such leaders – *informed allies* and *co-conspirators* are variant terms from contrasting trust chairpersons – must usually be engaged through a process. The objective is for them to make the case, the targets and the programme their own. Expect this to take time. There is an unstoppable urge with some charities to precede an appeal by dashing off a series of letters inviting powerful, busy people to chair it. Unsurprisingly, even where such an invitation comes from near the top of the establishment, this courts refusal. It is almost arrogant to assume that such people will without preparation take on the responsibility simply because an invitation comes from *this* address or charity. Such people have been extraordinarily busy during the past few years and have been receiving more charity invitations than during any previous period. Where there are exceptions and a swift acceptance comes, it may be because the person targeted is strongly predisposed towards the cause and the charity; because there is already a link and relationship; because there has in fact been surreptitious lobbying; or because this is a weak candidate, maybe with something to gain and little to lose.

A process for recruiting leaders which has frequently worked follows a process something like Figure 4.1.

1–3.   The early drafts of case, targets and lists are, for our purposes here, vehicles for gaining progressive

1. Draft case, targets, → 2. Private → 3. Revise drafts → (4. Steering group) →
plan, leadership   consultations   following
lists   consultation

5. Group briefings → 6. Nucleus of fund- → 7. Early funds → 8. Launch →
                        raising group

9. Follow-up   → 10. Consolidation

Figure 4.1

involvement both from the people who will provide access
to early leaders and from these early leaders themselves.
They are not invited to join anything; simply asked to
comment on arguments for an appeal, its financial
objectives, proposed strategy and some of the people being
considered for invitation to first-stage leadership. They are
unlikely to alter the drafts radically. If they do, pay
attention. Have they shown there to be the wrong case or
no case? Otherwise, revisions may be minor but important,
partly because they are likely to strengthen
communications but more importantly because they
indicate that these prospects are making the case their own.
When a few years ago the development director of a
national arts organisation phoned in alarm because the
clearing bank chairman being consulted was changing the
drafts, my advice was to have him chair the next steering
group meeting. He did so and soon chaired the appeal,
putting up the first pace-setting grant.

4.   The steering group is an option. It may be a necessary
      device to provide temporary leadership until qualified
      fund-raising leaders can be enlisted. It may become the
      body representing a charity's interests and providing
      oversight of progress on its behalf but without primary
      fund-raising responsibilities.

5.   To accelerate the process and the formation of active
      teams for fund-raising, short briefing sessions may be held
      on the case, targets and plan. These would probably not

last more than ninety minutes, with twenty minutes of presentation and the rest of the time available for the charity's staff and selected steering group members and early leaders to discuss issues and to listen, so that the views and predispositions of prospects can be remembered and reported afterwards.

6, 7. Out of such a process the nucleus of the main fund-raising group and also a chairperson may be enlisted. With the steering group for the arts organisation just mentioned, the chairman, having tabled £250,000, broke the meeting off halfway through the agenda to say: 'Let's now disband the steering group. Any of you who will give and ask for funds, please join my appeal committee.' Such a committee will bring itself up to strength to achieve coverage of its target prospects through the same kind of methods described at point 5 above. It may form subgroups to help achieve this. This fund-raising nucleus and its most direct contacts would be the sources for pre-launch pledges. The fund-raising group would also give authority to the appeal's fund-raising aids and materials.

8–10. The achievement at the time of the launch would give credibility to the targets. The follow-up would be personal and prompt. Consolidation has already been discussed.

Where this was relevant, all these processes would be paralleled locally or regionally. In such a case there may need to be a national fund-raising committee, perhaps meeting as the appeal starts, again mid-term and then when the results were delivered. The opening meeting can give reassurance and provide for coordination between sections of the appeal. Indeed, it can create productive competition. The mid-term meeting can see how different sections of the appeal might help each other, the national major support group perhaps boosting some regional activity. The final meeting, hopefully a celebration of success, also helps to build future consolidation.

I repeat that the process may be gradual and agonising. The Northern Ireland Voluntary Trust took eighteen months to two years before the first qualified leaders were found and convinced. The cause should have had priority and people gave lip-service to this, but they withheld real assent. The charity was new and started with no influential friends. It endured that process I have described. It is now one of the Province's great successes. This would not be the case if, prematurely and without adequate leadership, it had initiated large-scale fundraising.

Communications

This section of the book, and much that precedes it, concerns persuasive communication. Fund-raising represents one or more fields within that broad heading. It seems worthwhile to look at some basic points about communications, using two familiar models, because charities of all kinds so often communicate ineffectually. This stunts their fund-raising achievement. One reason is that charity people are often experts on a cause and on service delivery within it – or are at least familiar with these. For convenience and from familiarity, they often use jargon or shorthand communicating with colleagues inside and outside their organisation. They do not routinely spend time considering what the cause and their service mean to outsiders, to whom the insiders' assumptions and utterances may appear to be ill-founded or to be sloppy and incomplete. There may be particular danger of this in such fields as social work, ecology and medicine. (There may also be danger of this for the fundraising activity, which seems to want its own jargon, perhaps to boost confidence and a fake sense of professionalism: 'making the ask' instead of 'asking' is a horrible example of this.)

I have often said that good communication starts inside the head of the message's intended receiver. What are their knowledge, prejudices, perceptions, awareness and preferences? What is their current behaviour? These matters were discussed earlier as objects for research just as they are the common objects for research in marketing and advertising generally. The matters affected in designing communications touch all elements, from the message and the means for its delivery to the words, images, style and tone of voice.

Figure 4.2 shows an elementary model. My commentary is brief and assumes interactions between all elements in the

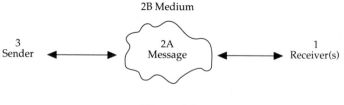

Figure 4.2

communication: sender and receiver; sender, message and receivers (do they receive what is sent?); sender, receiver and medium.

1. *Receivers* will have been selected for a specific purpose. Research will identify and characterise them so that the message can be framed in terms of their awareness, knowledge, attitudes, prejudices and capacities to respond. The sender will know what is to be achieved. The message is to evoke this.
2. *Message*: The message will give reasons and motives for the actions required: to act, to attend, to give, to join – whatever this may be. Note that even two, simultaneously delivered, non-contradictory messages can nullify each other.
3. *Medium*: Medium and message must work together. The medium can contradict the message or frustrate its delivery. The style of a function or document will be the first thing to strike the receiver's perceptions. Is the brochure too glossy? Too bland? Is the function too lavish (who has paid?) or too unwelcoming? Thus the medium itself influences reception of the message. It also affects senders: is this speaker inhibited by the platform, the microphone or the camera? Is the patron inept at writing letters? Are the staff shy at parties? Is the chairperson boring?

Where, for economy's sake perhaps, a single communication is directed at a number of different target groups, it may be effective only with one or be lost on all. A document apt for companies may be offputting to private individuals.

In Figure 4.3, the communication may well fail. Here, A, B and C are disparate target groups and there has been a false

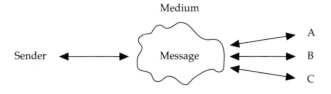

Figure 4.3

economy. However, in Figure 4.4 the communication may succeed. Here, A, B and C are disparate target groups; 1, 2 and 3 are messages designed for each.

That analysis of communication can help with its design and delivery. The following very ancient analysis, going back to classical rhetoric and transmitted in medieval and Reformation days through generations of preaching and speaking textbooks, can help to frame the message. At J. Walter Thompson, the advertising agency, it was called the *T Plan*. It assumes that the target group, the receivers, have been identified and described, and that the sender is clear what response is intended from them. (Messages should, I believe, be simple.)

The framework is as follows:

1. First level: *senses*. The non-reflective impression given by the communication which can be lost at this stage.
2. Second level: *intelligence*. The proposed reasons for the desired response.
3. Third level: *emotion and will*. To resolve the desired outcome and deliver the intended result.

I immediately note that the reasons given and the intended response can be fatuous: use this soap, buy this car, wear these jeans and you will be like *them* – the shining role models in the

Figure 4.4

commercial. Persuading somebody to become a name at Lloyd's used to include assurance of effortless profits but often with a significant added appeal to vanity. Similarly, does the coupon below the photograph of child famine victims rationally reassure me that my £50 will reach them? Or that it will do them good? Or that, when it arrives, it will still be £50 or even £45? Is it rational that I should give your appeal £100,000 because that is what you gave to mine? My point is not that messages and responses should all be rational. It is that the message should in many or even most cases allow for more than reason alone. There are apparent exceptions, where the proposition is to meet strict trust terms or to prove commercial benefit to a sponsor or joint promoter but even here there should be some allowance for imperfectly rational humanity.

Here is an application of the schema from the framework, adapted for promoting use of tax concessions.

- The message must receive first-level acceptance from the senses where it may be rejected at first glance or given further, more considered attention. Thus the message about the tax concession may be rejected because of the brown envelope carrying it, because it appears to be about tax and contracts, because it is too evidently an appeal or because, whatever its perceived content, it looks too complicated. It may succeed because it is immediately perceived to be about children or animals, because it is seen to be a personal letter or invitation from a friend or from somebody else respected by the recipient.

- The message must then receive second-level assent from reason. You must win the arguments for your cause and then for use of the tax concession as the means to give it support. In the abstract, your argument could aim to evoke some such reflection as this in the recipient: 'These needs are certainly urgent [this cause deserves support] and here is a charity whose programmes offer the services required. If these are to be effective, they must attract £1m [£100,000] from voluntary sources. They have asked me for £50,000 [£5,000], which will enable them to achieve this specified quantum of service. Such a gift from me would make a real difference in this situation. There are few people to whom they can look for such support. Unless I and others like me provide it, their programme will fail. It is this tax concession that makes it possible for me to make this gift. £10,000 [£1,000] yearly over the next four years – which can be paid in monthly instalments – will yield about £55,500 [£5,500] and is within my means. It will also enable me to associate personally with an organisation and people whom I respect.'

- The message will be ineffectual unless, at the third level, it evokes the required response from the emotions and will, taking the argument to a practical conclusion. Here sits the difference between notional and real assent. The outcome of the above ratiocination might be: 'I want to back this charity programme or cause using the tax concession of the size proposed. I must now take this action which I see is required to achieve this.'

There must be an available proposed way to respond: return an RSVP card, fill in a card asking for a phone-call or visit (which can increase the response) or fill in a form seeking further information. If the response is to attend a function or briefing, the event must be followed up promptly. Such follow-up is equivalent to the response device in direct marketing. Both recognise that, unless quickly reinforced, remembrance of the message and determination to respond will swiftly fade.[2]

Those models appear static. In life they can be made dynamic, without losing their essential shape. During the consultative stage of the process, in testing, after first objectives have been achieved – at any of these points receivers may change the message, as they themselves change. A medium (such as the foundation or a friends membership) may become the vehicle for consolidation and for sustaining relations with various categories of supporters, from friends and subscribers to patrons and foundation members. As the cycle should never be static, nor should a charity's communications.

Key points

- Major support for an appeal is usually best secured through personal peer approaches by leaders appropriately financially committed to the cause.

- Where there are leadership groups, these should meet. The appeal will be less successful if it is managed through isolated operators.
- Where there are several leadership and other groups, there may need to be a structure that coordinates and builds synergy between them.
- Communications must be designed skilfully and sensitively in relation to each target group at which they are aimed, with planned immediate and longer-term outcomes.

5 Increasing returns

Chapter summary

This chapter proposes a different model for planning, appraisal and management in complex fund-raising programmes. It is argued that a point can be reached in a funding programme where it will develop its own momentum, delivering *increasing returns*. Different elements within the appeal will reinforce each other increasingly productively. Multipliers can be introduced which stimulate such increasing returns and reinforcement. Principal factors in achieving this will be the techniques and organisation (*the frame*); the high and increasing targets proposed (*gearing*); the sequence of events and time allowed for the processes to develop; the emotional impact of the message, the leadership, the resources and the investment committed to the cause (*energy*). The outcomes of a programme that delivers increasing returns may not be rational. The process it engenders may be unstoppable. The process may also produce outcomes which, benevolent or malign, could not be predicted (*emergence*). Effective fund-raising changes the realities.

Increasing returns

In this section I offer a different approach to the analysis and appraisal of fund-raising. It starts with a *reprise*.

Causes and not-for-profit enterprises grow, nourished by fund-raising, in society (national, regional and international). This embraces people, governments, organisations and spontaneous groups: a complexity. Within society there are always unserved needs and gaps in the provision of services that people want. *Pace* current legislation, the Charity Commission and the CENTRIS report, there is also a need for groups that deal with the causes or roots of society's ills, being truly radical; but there should be no division between providers of services and radicals, since this is what gives realism to both. This may relate to the relief of sickness and poverty or the creation of an opera house or the establishment of a campaigning organisation. If the funding initiative and the particular response to need attract the concentrated concern and activity of sufficient people, the cause will begin to build its own magnetism and field of energy. *There is a point that this can reach at which the cause will begin to gather its own momentum, delivering increasing returns.* The process is not wholly rational or intelligible: why did anti-slavery causes reach a critical moment in the early nineteenth century and Third World causes in the 1960s? These movements passed a point beyond which they became unstoppable. *This can be shocking.*[1]

My purpose here is to see how a form of analysis, using an increasing-returns model, may improve strategic planning, management and post-evaluation for fund-raising. Initial concepts are these:

- *Increasing returns.* Beyond some point, there will be a strengthening of connections, activity and productivity.
- *Reinforcement*, which will take place within and between the constituent elements in the enterprise.
- *Multipliers,* which can be introduced to stimulate increasing returns and reinforcement.
- *Emergence.* Expect that an enterprise of this kind which develops successfully will generate its own, often unplanned outcomes. What worked before may perform differently next time. A successful enterprise will change the realities (including expectations and attitudes).

There are some cautions. The processes described are designed for growth. They are neutral of value. Some growth is undesirable. Nor is the process necessarily rational in its choices and development. In the commercial market-place, increasing returns may boost a product or process which is not the best available: the QWERTY keyboard, for example, or the VHS video system (against the allegedly better BETA). The point is that these developed an apparently unstoppable momentum, independently of their longer-term validity. There are many examples from voluntary enterprise. In the mid-1980s Giles Pegram (then Appeals Director at NSPCC) and I planned in terms of a *critical mass of support* which must be achieved for a total funding strategy to succeed. Beyond an indefinite point, the different parts of such a programme gather strength from each other. They generate energy independently of the case or needs. Chris Langton of the Santa Fe Institute, describing behaviour in a dynamic system, has said:

From the interaction of the individual components down here emerges some kind of global property up here, something you couldn't have predicted from what you know of the component parts. And the global property, this emergent behaviour, feeds back to influence the behaviour of the individuals down here that produced it.[2]

A fund-raising model

Figure 5.1 is a model based on the principles proposed. It presupposes a complex fund-raising universe, encompassing people with different means and attitudes; companies, trusts; national, local, regional; EU, government; and competitive voluntary enterprises of many kinds. It is not based on a philanthropic transaction between two people. It postulates these principal factors:

1. The frame: techniques and organisation.
2. Gearing: ratcheting performance upwards from its original bases; establishing productive scales of performance; setting (possibly unprecedentedly) high targets in relation to principal target sources' potential.
3. Time and the sequence of activities.
4. Energy: motive and message; leadership; investment; resources.

I shall discuss these factors through a series of illustrations and observations. First, note that there has to be a sufficient pool of potential to yield the results intended and that the motive and

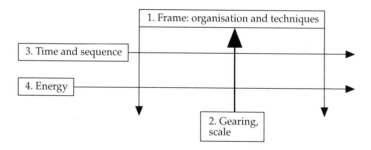

Figure 5.1

message (rational, emotional or both) must carry a charge of energy above some (unknown) minimum.

Organisation and techniques

Organisation and techniques refer to the structures for management, to involvement of staff and volunteers, and to the mixture of fund-raising methods used. A charity's fund-raising methods and organisation can exclude or obstruct potentially highly productive segments of support:

• A charity with outstanding performance in direct marketing and joint promotions with companies had no procedures, propositions or dedicated staff and resources to secure and sustain the kind of major support I have been discussing. Yet there was evidence that it could attract such support. When demand for increased income became acute and established methods reduced in yield, there was latent potential to be realised if the opportunity was grasped. This would entail the introduction of a leadership group with the accompanying staff, research and high-pitched propositions and programmes. Otherwise the charity would lack the means to make its due response to the needs it should serve.

• Most grant-making trusts are the vehicles used by rich families, individuals and some companies to deliver their gifts and grants. The most productive way to secure major support from these sources is through the kind of peer persuasion that has been described earlier. This process is best managed within a charity by staff with major support skills. Yet many charities create a trust department that functions fairly autonomously, appeals too often being signed by a trust development officer, clashing with and cutting across the charity's major support activity.

- Indeed, it is common to see approaches to major sources signed by a fund-raising operative rather than by the chairperson, director, a senior care specialist or some other more appropriate person.
- There may be many originating points for direct marketing within a charity which are uncoordinated and duplicate each other. In such a situation, inappropriate mail and other communications are most likely to reach major support prospects. This is not merely inefficient and exasperating, but it can also thwart and negate properly structured, major support approaches.
- There are programmes (including some famine appeals) with large impact where more segmented organisation and techniques and higher gearing could hugely increase the funds raised, provided that there were time for the anticipation required and techniques were in place to achieve such higher returns. In an undifferentiated mass appeal, it will be difficult to promote units of support much above £250. If lists and procedures were in place for this, many sums above £1,000 or £5,000 could be secured.
- The organisational structure may encourage leadership, if the development body gives the authority and status to its members. Or, if an inappropriate structure is imposed, the structure may demotivate and repel them. A recent instance of this subordinated the development group, which was made up of key local chairpersons who were financially committed at a very high level, to a committee chaired by a relatively junior manager whose members were uncommitted and of low financial standing.

Gearing

Gearing refers to a series of factors, starting with the levels at which unit targets are set. These should be realistically challenging for each source. Where there is productive segmentation of prospects and propositions, category by category (individuals, companies and trusts), and upward mobility between segments, the gearing becomes part of a charity's developing relationship with its supporters. Yet some appeals are designed to deliver results from high-value segments well below their potential because of the low funding levels initially proposed and because there are no structures or procedures to achieve progressive, increasing returns from the sources that have become engaged. A series of elementary principles is invoked here: you don't receive what you don't ask for; people and institutions don't know how much you need until you tell them; in a successful programme, units of support cluster around the sums projected and promoted for the appeal. A high-level prospect, meeting a charity's director at a distinguished reception, takes the cigar out of his mouth and demands: 'What do you want, then?' The director replies: 'Oh, only the pleasure of your company, Mr X.' Mr X returns to his office, takes the cigar out of his mouth and gives his instruction: 'The fool didn't ask for anything, so send £1,000.' He would have given £100,000. Finally, supporters given gratification from their support will continue their giving and increase it, if they are asked to and if there are the structure and invitation to achieve this.

Time and sequence

Time and sequence refer to issues fairly completely outlined already. The timetable must allow for the preparatory phases of fund-raising to build strongly, without forcing the gradual processes required for success. On the other hand, a programme can lose motivation and momentum if it becomes over-protracted, without achievement. The sequence imposed on the techniques deployed can, as has been shown, either put them in unproductive conflict or allow them to reinforce each other.

- There are enterprises that allow too little time for reinforcement and increasing returns to develop and which scramble the sequence of events, producing diminishing returns. They allow inadequate time for the recruitment, briefing and involvement of leaders and of staff. They hasten too fast and force low-yield techniques into conflict with those with higher potential, confusing and demotivating key categories of supporter.

- There are also appeals that, failing to stimulate early increasing returns, become unproductive because they continue too long without renewing the energy, in terms of the motivation, leadership and resources they should put through the system. For some, success becomes unattainable. Meetings become repetitive, unproductive and demoralising, with no renewal or revitalisation of membership. Positive measures are needed to counteract the depressing effects of an overprotracted timescale.

- A premature gala performance with a high entry charge can pre-empt major support from the individuals and companies who are invited and attend. That £500 memorial goblet (yielding £100 to the cause) can prevent a £50,000 gift if the goblet is offered before persuasion for the gift is complete. The sequence of propositions is crucial. Late in an appeal, both gala and goblet may have their place.

Energy

Energy is to some extent intangible where it relates to the will and commitment of the organisation to achieve its appeal goals. It is tangible where it relates to the investment and resources put into the appeal.

- A potentially successful enterprise may fail because the board and senior staff are hesitant in their support; because they do not believe in the need; because there is a gulf between board, senior management, service staff and the fund-raising staff and volunteers. This is where fund-raising is cast as a mechanical or quasi-magical function, disastrously separated from the cause which should give it energy. Where insufficient investment is made, an appeal will languish. I have had clients who launched a major appeal, not because the funds were needed for responsive

service or because they believed in the feasibility of the fund-
raising enterprise but because they decided to undertake a
major support programme as a hopefully productive
venture, in which they believed conditionally and to which
they were only provisionally committed.

- The concept signalled by 'energy' is complex. There are
  enterprises like RNLI and Guide Dogs for the Blind whose
  organisation has so much energy that they continue
  gathering funds regardless of the objective needs. There have
  been appeals sparked by emotional events such as the East
  Coast floods or the loss of the Mousehole lifeboat, which
  created funds well in excess of the needs (except that the
  latter ignored the merchant ship's crew and their families),
  not requiring organisation and techniques for fund-raising
  (but lacking them for administration), where the energy was
  so intense that it gathered funds as into a tornado.

Applications

I suggest some other applications of the increasing-returns
model, to encourage its wider extension. It has helped with
decision when there was a dilemma in the execution of strategy.
A strong leader was prepared to put great energy through a
weak technique but would put none through one that was
known to be stronger. Our question: will it be more productive
to shed the leader and deploy the strong technique with
leadership from someone weaker but more willing to comply?
Or to retain the strong leader on the grounds that great energy
will override a technique's weaknesses? The choice was to retain
the leader whose energy was stronger. We may have been
wrong.

Quite evidently, this model provides a framework, albeit
fallible, for judgement: about the timing, in relation to a fund-
raising launch and for putting the staff and volunteer leadership
in place; about the levels at which funding propositions should
be pitched; about investment.

The increasing-returns model can also help interpretation of
past success, opportunity or failure. One programme I worked
with recently had set a sensible budget and timetable; its appeal

was succeeding but (during the recession) returns were delayed. By continuing investment, an additional £2–4m could have been gained; but the finance department insisted that there should be no deviation from the original financial plan. There had been a success. There could have been a victory. That model might have provided the analysis and persuasion needed to change fixed investment decisions so that there was a fuller realisation of the charity's available potential support.

On the other hand, I also see agencies that should be allowed to die, which are sustained like headless chickens by their residual energy.

Emergence

What, then, of *emergence*? It is an outcome of the connections and the relationships postulated by this model. It presupposes that energy will come from the people involved through their personal and financial commitment. This must include main categories of backers, who should be involved in articulating the messages and transmitting the motivation, but without hijacking or compromising the ideals or values of the enterprise. Key backers will have impact on the case and the productive contacts. They should also be involved in reinforcement of the enterprise beyond the period of an intense appeal (unless this is for a one-off objective). They should be principal multipliers securing increasing returns for the enterprise in the future, provided that this is still something society needs. They will do this if they are allowed full and growing satisfaction from their support.

There is a common-sense aspect to emergence which can easily be ignored. NSPCC's 1984 success was used as a model in many other appeals. Great Ormond Street adapted it and delivered further trend-setting results. NSPCC built on its achievement. Other charities that thought they were adopting a formula for success were disappointed in their results. Some of them deserved to be: they under-invested and committed scant corporate will to their enterprises. Others achieved lower results for reasons stemming directly from the NSPCC, Wishing Well and Prince's Youth Business Trust successes. These had changed funders' attitudes and behaviour, so that nothing could be the same again. In a small country with a finite number of financially potent individuals and institutions, they had engaged and thereby qualified the future impact of a generation of fund-raising leaders. A new generation was emerging even as this happened. There were new successes and few real excuses, except that the United Kingdom endured the worst recession in most of our lifetimes.

However, I suspect that productive emergence in performance and relationships – outside the anticipated likely achievements of the strategies we plot – is something we must be prepared to accommodate. We should be constructively open to surprise. *Effective fund-raising changes the realities.*

Key points

- Fund-raising programmes on a certain scale can be designed so that they may be able to gather the critical mass that enables them to deliver *increasing returns*.
- This means that, with main parts of the programme reinforcing each other, they begin and continue to perform well beyond what is normal, in terms of levels of support and numbers of sources participating.
- To achieve this there must be the techniques and organisation (*frame*); the challenging targets (*gearing*); an apt sequence of events and sufficient time allowed; the motivation, leadership, resources and investment (*energy*) that will allow this to happen.
- A fund-raising programme that delivers increasing returns may have unforeseen outcomes for the charity and for the world of fund-raising (*emergence*).

6 Two case studies: NSPCC and NIVT

These case studies have been selected because they both reflect over ten years of achievement. This is a timespan that allows the full working out of a strategy. They are also for contrasting organisations: one long established, the other newborn when we started working together.

The NSPCC's centenary: a case study

Principles established

Nineteen-eighty-four was centenary year for Britain's main movement working for the prevention of cruelty to children. The anniversary provided no reason in itself that anybody should pay special attention or give extraordinarily generously. It was an opportunity, though, that the Society could exploit if it chose to do so. It could be made the occasion for a reappraisal and reaffirmation of roles and services. It could be used to increase public understanding of issues relating to cruelty to children. It could be marked by a major fund-raising drive to raise a significant amount during the centenary year and to increase NSPCC's long-term skills and resources for fund-raising.

In 1980, when the decisions were made, NSPCC was well known and respected. The issues it addressed and its services were fairly poorly understood and the Society's image was old-fashioned, respectable and dull. It lacked the funds to fulfil its full role on behalf of children at risk or to develop and improve its response to their needs. There was an operating deficit of £1m. NSPCC's income was then just £5m. Its greatest fund-raising strength was a nationwide network of voluntary committees, successful in fund-raising through coffee mornings, social events and other such methods. Income from trading, direct donors, corporate sources and big gifts was minimal. In this it resembled many of the United Kingdom's major national charities.

The decision was taken to exploit the opportunity and to exploit it boldly. During October 1980, the Society's trustee body appointed a centenary steering sub-committee which had its first meeting.

In December, Giles Pegram (Appeals Director) retained me to work with him as fund-raising consultant on planning the centenary appeal.

From the start, there was an explicit intention to create a quantum leap in the fund-raising performance of one of Britain's great, old, established, underperforming charities. There had to be some bold, responsible affirmations. The first concerned the NSPCC itself. We reckoned that the Society's history and role established a cause that could draw attention from everybody in Britain and that the NSPCC could secure support from a high proportion of the total population. We judged that the Society had authority to engage the most powerful leadership in the land. We acknowledged that this would entail some very major changes within NSPCC.

If these assumptions were right, there was the basis for an extraordinary plan. It could only work:

- if there was a target that would challenge staff, volunteers and donors (overlapping groups) to unprecedented levels of performance and generosity;
- if the plan was bold, pioneering and inspiring;
- if the Society's self-perception and performance were both significantly uplifted;
- if the timescale, investment and single-minded commitment to succeed by the NSPCC allowed for achievement.

There were two other crucial premises. The first was that the centenary appeal had to engage the most powerful financial and social leadership locally as well as nationally. The second was that, as far as time and resources permitted, all target prospects would be offered *multiple, ordered, cumulative opportunities for giving – within a concerted strategy.*

The financial aims would be to secure a very substantial, one-off figure during centenary year and also to build NSPCC's skills, structures, procedures and resources to achieve greatly enhanced income in later years.

The centenary fund-raising plan or strategy had to allow for the numbers and quality of the Society's existing fund-raising staff, groups and volunteers. Normal activities were to be integrated with the centenary activities. This had to be achieved while new structures, staff and volunteers were introduced to secure new types and levels of funding. Crucial elements in centenary strategy were perceived to be as follows:

- A national committee to coordinate and give authority to the overall programme.
- A committee to engage the most powerful national leaders in NSPCC's centenary fund-raising, aimed at companies, major grant-making trusts and wealthy individuals.
- A network of significantly powerful new committees throughout the country to make approaches for support to companies, trusts and wealthy individuals locally.
- The strengthening of NSPCC's internal resources for fund-raising through, for example, sponsorships, promotions, special events, direct mail and other central initiatives.
- The development of PR and advertising to build awareness and to complement and reinforce main fund-raising activities.
- Provision for post-centenary consolidation of what was to be gained during 1984.

Achievement would require advocacy for the NSPCC from powerful, committed leaders nationally and locally. The programme would not work without a concerted strategy to create synergy between its parts. This in turn required an organisational and communications structure that would permit management and coordination to work effectively. Every sector of the appeal must have its activity and target. Staff and volunteers would need the training, motivation and support to carry the programme through.

This was the first time that a major national charity in the United Kingdom had undertaken such a programme.

Preliminaries

During 1981, experiments were carried out in four locations to test the concept of local big-gift campaigns and to establish organisers' requirements for training and support (organisers are the Society's local fund-raising staff). There were discussions and training exercises with selected staff. These led in September to the definition of a senior officer's role for the centenary. There was an audit of records and an appraisal of previous corporate fund-raising. Strategy was refined. By the end of 1981, Pegram and I had completed basic planning for the following:

- A corporate committee capable of covering all sectors of commerce and industry comprehensively and in depth. There were twelve main sectors. Leaders for each would be enlisted from one of the five strongest companies in each sector. Redmond Mullin Ltd produced the first draft corporate contact list, arranged by sectors, to assist the enlistment of corporate leaders.
- A network of new area committees, to operate in parallel with existing volunteer groups. The organisers responsible for old and new committees would receive training and supplementary support for this.
- A national centenary committee with thirty members, including twelve sector heads from the corporate committee and nine local representatives of the area committees, the balance representing sport, the media, youth and other special interests.
- The Duke of Westminster had been identified as the most eligible chairperson for the appeal and had accepted the invitation.
- A vice-chairperson was to be drawn from the key corporate leaders.

Between January and May 1982, Redmond Mullin Ltd had worked with NSPCC staff to define criteria and procedures for the enlistment of area chairpersons. A training programme for organisers had been devised. Guidelines had been established for research into grant-making trusts. The key corporate contact lists had been revised and profiles made of the Society's trustees to map their possible contacts with the corporate individuals thus identified.

A crucial planning meeting with the Duke of Westminster took place in June 1982. It involved Dr Gilmour (Director of NSPCC), Giles Pegram, the new organiser for industry and trusts and myself. Main topics for the meeting were as follows:

1. The prospect lists of early possible leaders.
2. A draft strategic timetable for the centenary.
3. A proposal for sector targets as follows:

(a)	national industry and commerce	£4m
(b)	regional committees	£4m
(c)	wealthy individuals	£1m
(d)	trusts and foundations, distinct from (a) and (c)	£500,000
(e)	public appeals and national organisations/ youth	£2m
(f)	sponsorships and promotions	£500,000
	Total provisional target	£12m

    Note: It was accepted at this stage that £12m could be pruned to £10m if emergent facts justified this.
4. Preliminary objects for the appeal, in terms of the prevention of cruelty to children.
5. The national committee structure, with a vice-chairperson from industry.

The main action following this meeting in June 1982 was the selection from prepared lists of a proposed nucleus for the corporate committee, who were to be invited for a meeting at the Duke of Westminster's Grosvenor Estate offices on 22 September. During July, a regular series of meetings began between the Duke of Westminster, the staff coordinating team and Redmond Mullin Ltd. This was to continue into 1985.

During July, August and September 1982, preparatory activity was consolidated. A panel was formed to advise on Friends of the NSPCC, a quasi-membership scheme, to add a new tier to the Society's body of regular supporters. The Friends promotion and related magazine were in an advanced stage by September. The first in a series of briefing papers, primarily aimed at area committees and organisers, defined the period July–December 1982 with the slogan: 'Phase One – Finding the People'. A simplified linear timetable was given and emphasis was on enlistment. The Lord Mayor of London elect confidentially indicated during July that she would adopt NSPCC as the specially favoured charity for her year of office.

The corporate meeting on 22 September was a turning point for the campaign. Sir Maurice Laing (of John Laing PLC, major builders) was one of the four who attended, together with the Chairman of Barclays Bank. The main decision was that Margaret Thatcher should be asked to hold a reception at 10 Downing Street during the spring of 1983, with Princess Margaret, NSPCC's president, as guest of honour. The objective would be to bring the corporate committee and its subgroups up to strength, so that all sectors of industry and commerce could be powerfully, personally canvassed on NSPCC's behalf. Over the following weeks, the Duke of Westminster met separately with other potential leaders, including Gerald Ronson of Heron International. (Thus both future vice-chairpersons were involved at a very early stage.)

As volunteers and staff became active in their various functions and roles, separate parts of the programme developed their own dynamic, always within the scope of the master strategy and under clear management direction. I therefore think that my treatment of the final preparatory phase will be more coherent if its parts are studied separately and then put back into context. First, the 10 Downing Street enlistment event will be treated continuously.

During October, Margaret Thatcher responded to a letter from the Duke of Westminster by agreeing to a 10 Downing Street reception for 5 May 1983. Already in September corporate sectional prospect lists had been extended. The nucleus of the committee and others associated with the Society were engaged in this process of identification and contact. Draft documentation for the corporate appeal was amended. On 9 February 1983 there was a meeting of the industrial committee which agreed the following:

- that 10 Downing Street was for 'askers' (not donors);
- that these 'askers' would also in time be big givers;
- that lists of prospective guests would be thoroughly vetted by the committee.

The 9 February meeting was followed by private meetings involving, among others, Vivien Duffield (Sears and the Clore Foundation), Lord Forte (Trusthouse Forte), Lord Aldington (Westland Helicopters and Sun Alliance) and Lord Weinstock (GEC). By 11 March a priority list of 100 guests had been drafted and a back-up list prepared and put in order of priority. The coordinating group met with the Duke on 22 March. Follow-up letters to all categories of possible attenders and non-attenders were drafted in April.

An industrial committee on 12 April meeting could therefore have been seen as disastrous, given the stakes then on the table. Only Sir Maurice Laing attended. He saved the occasion. The minutes showed, accurately, that five of the eleven required sector leaders were in place. Sectors were to include ten influential 'askers' each. A further home team briefing meeting was scheduled for 5 May. This was eventually held at Downing Street. Sir Maurice gave authority to the decisions that had to be made by the committee and a number of other key decisions were made. The minutes failed to include details of who had attended the meeting that made these decisions!

The briefings issued to the home team and Prime Minister stressed that the reception was an enlistment, not a fund-raising occasion. Even on the night of the event, key figures had to be deflected from making an appeal. A meeting with the Duke of Westminster on 27 April resolved the final details for statements to be issued for attendees and non-attendees. The following scale of gifts was considered for those attending:

Number of gifts		Scale
1	×	£300,000 to £500,000
2	×	£200,000 to £300,000
5	×	£100,000 to £200,000
15	×	£50,000 to £100,000
20	×	£20,000 to £50,000
30	×	£10,000 to £20,000

On 5 May, fifty-nine major corporate heads, with partners, came to 10 Downing Street. Responsibility for each guest had been assigned to a member of the home team. Margaret Thatcher, a former trustee of NSPCC, endorsed the Society's work and positively encouraged guests to join the corporate fund-raising

committee for the centenary. Although enlistment was the theme for the evening, indications of the first three six-figure gifts emerged during the reception.

Follow-up was immediate and thorough. Two letters had been prepared for every guest expected; one assuming that they actually attended, the other that they had not. The appropriate letter was sent the morning after the reception. All members of the home team were debriefed the next day or soon after. There were follow-up interviews with E.R. Nixon of IBM, Sir Hector Laing of United Biscuits, Lord Forte and David Sieff. Through David Sieff, Sir Terence Conran was contacted. On being invited to accept leadership of the retail sector, he commented that by this stage it was like being asked to join the Cabinet. Further detailed follow-up was agreed at an industrial committee meeting on 12 May. Thus the 10 Downing Street reception put in place the strongest possible corporate committee to drive and lead this part of NSPCC's centenary programme.

No. 10 Downing Street was an important part of a far more extensive whole. In January 1983, there was a highly motivating meeting between all area chairpersons and the Duke at his West End office. His Grace also hosted a reception there for a large body of people who could help with publicity, promotion and events. Early during 1983, the first edition of *Centenary Stop Press* was published. This communication tool for staff and volunteers was issued quarterly throughout the campaign. The Friends scheme was launched at the end of April.

The national committee meeting on 12 May was therefore very positive. Forty-five out of sixty area chairpersons were in position, and seven out of nine regional representatives had been appointed. Thirty national organisations had committed their support. Young League's 'Give an Hour to a Child' was on schedule. Events at Ascot and Covent Garden had been agreed. There was to be a Kensington Palace reception in the autumn of 1983. Half the area committees had committed themselves to their targets, and the first eight pledges to the corporate committee totalled £685,000. Saatchi & Saatchi had completed their dummy brochure. Perhaps most importantly, the Society's centenary charter, defining future priorities for the protection of children, was presented, giving solid and visionary grounds for the appeal.

June 1983 was a period of significant consolidation:

- The area committee chairpersons met alone on their own initiative. They formed a competitive, mutually supportive determination to succeed.
- Following an ill-attended meeting, the corporate committee resolved to meet monthly and insist on solid attendance.
- Sir Mark Weinberg became Treasurer of the NSPCC and a pattern of regular meetings was established between Gerald Ronson, Sir Maurice Laing, NSPCC staff and Redmond Mullin Ltd.
- With the appointment of Derek Robertson to a new senior post responsible for the corporate committee, other staff were released to concentrate on foundations and other key sources. At the same time, training, monitoring systems, records and central controls were all strengthened.
- The consultants stressed the need for some major gifts (£300,000, £500,000, £1m). It considered gaps in centenary coverage, especially in relation to the individually wealthy. It also recommended consideration of the structure and procedures to consolidate the centenary achievement beyond 1984.

Advanced preparations were completed during July and August, with corporate and area committees building their strength and resources. The PR strategy for the centenary was presented by public relations agency Dewe Rogerson during August. Project and network research were used continuously to feed the committees with data on sources. By September the corporate committee had secured ten pledges between £50,000 and £150,000, yielding something over £1m. This, the consultants pointed out, suggested an end achievement below £4m; therefore there should be some concentration on objects and sources targeted between £200,000 and £1m. A luncheon at 10 Downing Street was proposed as one method for securing such support. A strategy for the long-term involvement of certain individuals, nationally and locally, beyond the centenary had now been tabled.

The national committee met on 12 October. The Duke of Westminster was able to show that the main centenary structure was now in place and that the campaign was on schedule.

Sir Mark Weinberg went round the room asking each member to indicate their own target. He added the totals up on his pocket calculator. Most importantly, the divisional representatives committed themselves to targets in excess of £4m and the meeting affirmed a total centenary target of £12m. This was now the committees' own target, not a figure imposed by the Society. This was critical. Up to this point the staff and consultants had been driving the committee. From this point on the committee and its officers drove themselves!

The centenary appeal

The centenary appeal was launched to the press on 18 October 1983.

On the evening of 27 October, Princess Margaret gave a reception at Kensington Palace for major national organisations and selected foundation trustees and directors. The 120 guests who attended were followed up to establish how best they could support the appeal. A fairly small proportion became actively involved but these few gave substantial backing to the appeal (for example, the National Association for Flower Arranging Societies actually contributed a six-figure sum).

During November, it was agreed that the corporate committee's affairs should be routinely managed by two vice-chairpersons. These posts would be filled by Sir Maurice Laing and Gerald Ronson. Saatchi & Saatchi submitted their advertising plan for 1984. On 12 November, the NSPCC float in the Lord Mayor's Show was the first public event of the centenary. Also during November, the ideas forum had the first of its monthly meetings to appraise suggested initiatives; this involved NSPCC staff and their consultants.

By December, staff and voluntary groups were poised to implement the strategy. The area committees had targeted themselves to raise a new £4,790,000 against a budget of £4m. Corporate committee pledges had reached £1,901,850 and there were strong subcommittees working in, for example, the retail and construction sectors. Plans for further resource events at 10 Downing Street and Claridges had been agreed.

As the year ended, a gap analysis was carried out by staff

with Redmond Mullin Ltd. This considered weak corporate and professional sectors as well as wealthy individuals and local sources. A searching questionnaire was ready for despatch to field staff, to help them understand their position and to enable headquarters to make tactical intervention where this would be constructive. Procedures for acknowledging gifts and for giving donors adequate recognition were being planned.

• One major feature of the centenary was the extraordinary activity of Princess Margaret and of the Duke of Westminster, who criss-crossed the country throughout 1984 on the Society's behalf.
• Another was the commitment of the voluntary committees and their fruitful mutual interaction.
• Finally, there was the Society's single-minded commitment to the plan, in terms of staff, policy and investment.

Working within specific corporate sectors or other networks of peer contact, the corporate committee met monthly, Sir Maurice Laing and Gerald Ronson chairing alternate meetings. The Duke attended periodically.

During January and February the corporate committee had defined three key resource events for fund-raising. The Prime Minister confirmed that she would give a dinner party for forty couples at 10 Downing Street on 19 June. The Society aimed to raise £1m from those attending. There were also to be receptions at the New Berkeley Hotel, with Princess Margaret in attendance, and at the Mansion House, in the presence of Lady Donaldson, the Lord Mayor. Sir Maurice Laing announced that John Laing PLC had challenged its staff to match, pound for pound, £100,000 from the board. Robert Maxwell initiated a media subcommittee at proprietor and chief executive level. In March it was announced that Princess Margaret would host a dinner party at Kensington Palace on 22 November for up to sixteen guests.

At the April meeting, some corporate sectors were approaching their targets, while others were lagging behind. Strong sectors therefore began to assist those that were weaker. Two and a half million pounds had been pledged. The Laing employee fund-raising drive had already achieved £60,000. Following a successful meeting with Rupert Murdoch, Robert

Maxwell's media advisory committee began its main phase of activity.

At the beginning of June the corporate committee had achieved £3.2m against a £5m target. Jocelyn Stevens took responsibility for coordinating sponsors and advertisers for a major Covent Garden gala.

On 19 June, the Prime Minister held her select dinner party. Guests had been meticulously selected and primed for the occasion, which was aimed at the top levels of wealth. During the evening the Japanese philanthropist Ryarichi Sasakawa presented a cheque for £500,000 to the Society.

Hence, by the July meeting, the corporate committee had achieved £4.65m against a revised £5.5m goal. By October £5.4m had been attained. This had risen to £5.8m in November. The corporate committee extended itself well beyond narrow sector responsibilities.

- It backed sponsorship and promotion initiatives.
- It supported Vivien Duffield's royal gala at Covent Garden.
- It backed Young League's 'Give an Hour to a Child'.
- Through John Laing PLC's campaign, it demonstrated what could be achieved through employee fund-raising. By September, Laing's staff had raised £114,895 through covenants, events and sponsored activities against the board's £100,000 challenge. In September, Sir Maurice said that the company had increased its matching funds to £250,000, so the drive could be targeted at £500,000. It achieved over £600,000. Sir Maurice offered the key executive involved, John Farrow, to help other companies wanting to mount similar schemes.
- The corporate committee's work was backed by strong staff support, led and directed by Derek Robertson.

Area committees were active throughout and beyond 1984. This part of the campaign was based on sixty-three committees, aimed at harnessing key leadership throughout the country, supplementing the work already done by NSPCC's existing groups. An extraordinary diversity and intensity of activity was achieved.

Area committees were most active during June, July and August (deliberately, a period of concentrated publicity for the

Society's work). Thus a £900,000 achievement by early April turned into a £5m success by 18 December. Throughout, counsel, resources and active intervention were provided from headquarters to area staff and volunteers.

During July 1983, foundations had been carefully subdivided between large, medium and small; local and national; general and specialised. Responsibility for them was given to the corporate or local committees, where there might be personal contact and influence, except where it was judged that a direct approach from, say, the Society's Director would be most effective. Progress was carefully monitored, so that foundations could be pulled back for central intervention where delegated responsibility was not being fulfilled. The total raised from trusts and wealthy individuals, as this part of the appeal was designated, was £764,000 against a £1m target.

There was an extensive programme of events:

- Both Princess Margaret and the Prime Minister spoke at NSPCC's AGM on 16 May, Margaret Thatcher announcing a substantial increase in the Society's statutory grant.
- Also during May, Terry Wogan opened the long-term Copper Mountain event at Selfridges. This would quickly become the world's largest pile of coins, which were collected in store and at police stations and other centres around the country.
- The thanksgiving service at St Paul's Cathedral was attended by Her Majesty the Queen, as patron of the Society.
- A gala performance of the *Nutcracker* ballet, sponsored through the corporate committee to £375,000 and targeted to net £500,000, was held in the presence of Her Majesty the Queen, the Duke of Edinburgh, the Queen Mother, Princess Margaret and Prince Andrew, with the Duke and Duchess of Westminster in attendance.
- A multitude of events around the country raised five- and six-figure sums.

All of this helped to keep NSPCC in public consciousness during the centenary. This was part of a carefully planned publicity campaign involving Saatchi & Saatchi for advertising and Dewe Rogerson for PR. There was massive press coverage during the key campaigning months of June, July and August 1984. There were also a number of coups:

- Late in January, Dewe Rogerson started discussion with *The Archers* – a popular, long-running radio soap opera in the United Kingdom – to discuss whether the Duke of Westminster might address their fictitious Borsetshire committee. When the programme went out on 22 May, Princess Margaret herself walked in as an unexpected guest. This was unprecedented in UK broadcasting.
- On 12 April, there was a leader in *The Times* on the Society and its work.
- Robert Maxwell's and Rupert Murdoch's papers gave positive backing to the appeal.
- *Private Eye* used one 'Dear Bill' letter to satirise the Downing Street dinner.

There was also an award-winning advertising campaign. The timing and content of these PR and advertising programmes were carefully pre-planned.

From the earliest stages of the active appeal, the national committee coordinated progress and was the place where intended synergy between diverse elements in the campaign was achieved. There were four meetings: in May 1983, October 1983, July 1984 and January 1985.

Their course marks progress of the campaign. The 12 May 1983 theme, to encourage committed engagement of committees in the programme, was 'Creating the Plan'. This was also the theme of the second briefing leaflet. In July 1984, by which time a total of £7.25m had been raised, the theme was 'Working Together for £12 Million'. When the fourth and final meeting was held at Claridges on 9 January 1985, pledges totalled £13,120,000 against the £12m target. This was an occasion for the Duke of Westminster to thank everybody who had worked so effectively on the appeal.

In the background there had been continuous monitoring by staff and Redmond Mullin Ltd. There had also been detailed work, not only on recognition of centenary appeal supporters, but also on consolidation of relations with certain of them. The consultants tabled a draft instrument for a national development body in February 1984. The final outcome of these recommendations would be the creation of a national financial development board, with strong staff support, to retain the quality of corporate advocacy which had been achieved during the centenary. Gradually it would also result in the establishment of child protection team support groups around the country, to consolidate equivalent local leadership for the future. The first of a series of donor receptions was held to build relationships with supporters.

There was also a final gap analysis. Key sources that had not responded were referred back to the Duke of Westminster or to selected members of his committees.

Inevitably it was found that a number of wealthy individuals had been missed by the campaign, so the year ended with a well-planned but unprecedented cold mailing seeking £1,000 or more from well-researched lists of prospects. This yielded a normal response for cold mailings and an average gift of £873, excluding one gift of £100,000 and one of £25,000.

The most important short-term effect of the campaign was that it enabled NSPCC to realise its centenary charter, deploying an improved network of child protection teams around the country. In immediate financial terms, by April 1985 the result looked like Table 6.1.

Consolidation

The long-term outcome of the NSPCC appeal has been even more impressive than the immediate result, but nothing on this

Table 6.1

Category	Target	Result
Area committees	£4m	£5,564,444
Corporate committee		
(a) Gifts	£4m	£5,786,276
(b) Sponsorships and promotions	£1m	£582,500
Trusts and individuals	£1m	£764,000
Public appeals and events	£2m	£1,662,200
Total	£12m	£14,359,420

scale would have developed without the discipline of the thoroughly planned and structured, total fund-raising campaign. Other charities in the United Kingdom mounted programmes with similar aims. Some were successful. Others failed because they did not make the same single-minded commitment to a concerted campaign or because they could not bring themselves to make the appropriate investment of resources, with acceptance of the fact that there must for a period be a net outflow of funds with no immediate prospect of a return.

NSPCC's voluntary income is now about £40m per annum, compared with £5m in 1980. This also puts the £15m centenary attainment in proportion. Since the early 1980s it had been reiterated to a sceptical inner group that the 1984 result would be dwarfed by what followed (see Figure 6.1).

An account of NSPCC's recent years would need a detailed history. The point to make here is that the Society sustained the

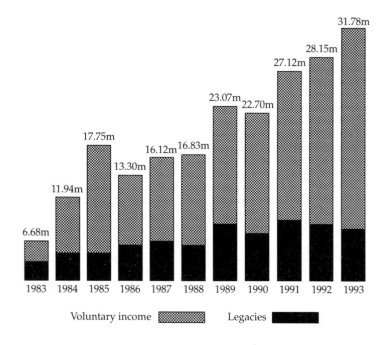

Figure 6.1

productive procedures introduced during the centenary. Segmentation of regular supporters was refined. The financial development board was in place to deliver £5m for the Leicester Training Centre. A series of contacts with supporters was introduced. Staff were assigned to main supporters, to provide a personal bridge in these key relationships. There has been a continuing programme for staff training and development.

None of this happened by accident. It was planned.

The NIVT: a case study

Note: David Cook's extensive contribution to this study is drawn from his paper to ICFM's 1991 Convention. The Institute has published a tape of his speech.

In 1979, there were virtually no indigenous grant-making trusts in Northern Ireland and such as there were, were very small. Although some UK trusts had an excellent record of grant-making in Northern Ireland, the funds that such trusts might have provided were as or more urgently needed in Northern Ireland than anywhere else in the United Kingdom. There was thought to be, on a strict per capita calculation, a below average contribution from British-based trusts, companies and rich individuals for voluntary action in Northern Ireland, where it could have had exceptional impact. Through an enlightened initiative Lord Melchett, encouraged and supported by Norman Dugdale (Permanent Secretary) and Maurice Hayes (Under Secretary), delivered initial endowment and impetus for development when, as a junior minister, he secured a founding fund of £500,000 from the Labour government of the time, with £250,000 in pound-for-pound challenge funding, thus establishing the Northern Ireland Voluntary Trust. The £500,000 was committed only days before Labour lost the election.

The first trustees were selected, 'to represent a cross-section of Northern Ireland's population with a strong bias in favour of those experienced in community development'. It was noteworthy 'that in selecting Trustees their fundraising potential . . . was *not* a primary consideration'. The chairman, David Cook, was a young solicitor experienced in public affairs who, in his thirties, became the first non-Unionist Mayor of Belfast. He later became deputy leader of Northern Ireland's Alliance Party. He remains as chairman of NIVT today. David was first approached early in the autumn of 1978 by Lord Melchett's private secretary. 'The boss has a job for you,' he was told. When he heard what was entailed he responded that he needed it 'like a hole in the head'. He then got to work. He pressed for the initial endowment of £500,000 (£250,000 had originally been suggested) as well as the £250,000 challenge fund. He also insisted that the trustees would be of critical importance. His colleagues must have street credibility in Northern Ireland's communities.

The Trust's first director was Hugh Frazer. Having worked for the Northern Ireland Council for Social Service (now the Northern Ireland Council for Voluntary Action), he had sound experience of the fields in which NIVT was to operate and of the issues that would have to be faced. With support from their trustees and a staff of one, David and Hugh drove and managed NIVT through its vulnerable early years.

Previous experience of grant-making into Northern Ireland had been patchy but above all it had been ephemeral. The Peace People Movement and others had raised enormous goodwill and attracted some significant funds in the 1970s. The quality and scale of other funding to voluntary enterprise in Northern Ireland had been uneven. Such experience confirmed the need to establish an indigenous endowment for Northern Ireland. So NIVT was created for reasons of policy:

- As an independent 'seeding grant' mechanism for small-scale, high-risk self-help projects.
- As a conduit for encouraging philanthropic funds into Northern Ireland in a highly complex political situation.

From the start, the trustees decided that there should be a small professional team to administer the Trust; and that through publication of its annual report and other publicity, NIVT would operate in the public domain. Trustees were to be actively engaged in the affairs of the Trust, individually and as a group, working closely with staff and other professionals.

The first annual report and the kind of body it should reflect were carefully considered. In terms of achievement, the Trust did not yet exist. It had quickly to project itself as skilled and sensitive in its grant-making and as the most apt and dependable body through which support could be given to certain kinds of voluntary activity in Northern Ireland, within and between its communities. It had been decided to back a small, carefully selected batch of initiatives, to establish a track record and thus to build understanding and credibility with beneficiaries and potential funders. It was recognised that the concept of the Trust might be difficult to comprehend. That first report, deliberately designed to look as if it was from an established corporate body, already illustrated the kinds of benefit that could distinctively be delivered through the Trust.

In 1980, following a competitive process, NIVT appointed me as fund-raising consultant to the project. The first question was whether the Trust could raise the funds to meet its £250,000 challenge from government. My advice was to start on a course that could eventually deliver £5m for Northern Ireland causes. The decision to invest in fund-raising was deliberate: 'to speculate to accumulate'.

The consultants presented their first, draft report in November 1980. This reflected a general welcome inside Northern Ireland for creation of the Trust, provided that it created new funding and did not divert funds from established agencies. There was a convergence of views between Protestant and Roman Catholic respondents to the study which was unexpected by the consultants. There was resistance from some individuals to the suggestion that funds might be attracted from the Republic. Generally, however, the initiative was welcomed in Northern Ireland, provided that it did not become a threat to other agencies and that it did deliver new support, sensitive to the many polarities there. The consultants also heard scepticism whether the Trust could ever attract the funds it would need to have serious impact on the issues.

There were other considerations. There was a scarcity of voluntary funds in Northern Ireland. The report commented that 'Statutory funding was seen as biased and in some ways tainted, for example it could not be obtained to meet certain urgent requirements of prisoners' families.' It was also reported that within government it was felt that, where they took action directly, sickly plants grew in the voluntary sector, experiment was difficult, action was inhibited by strict government controls. There were cumbersome problems in crossing departmental boundaries and the initiatives receiving support tended to be of the kind favoured by the conservative establishments.

The requirement for the new Trust was thus made clear from all concerned parties.

Decisions on corporate funding were mostly taken far away in London. In any case, as the report commented, 'in Britain there is a fairly well-established apathy or scepticism concerning new initiatives' for Northern Ireland. This stemmed from

boredom, disillusionment and a feeling of helplessness in relation to Northern Ireland's affairs. It is difficult to establish whether low awareness and consciousness of the real situation in Northern Ireland is a cause or effect of these attitudes . . . In Britain . . . there could be scepticism concerning the effectiveness of aid offered to Northern Ireland, and ignorance, boredom and reluctance to pay attention to the unpleasant, close realities embodied in the Northern Ireland problem . . .

This was at a time when Peter Townsend's *Poverty in the United Kingdom* (Penguin, 1979) demonstrated that, in relation to all major criteria of poverty, poverty was worse in Northern Ireland than anywhere else in the United Kingdom: lowest average incomes; 20 per cent unemployment; more than one-third of families in overcrowded, unfit housing; infant deaths at 20.2 per 1,000 against a 14 per 1,000 norm; well-above-average energy costs; all this compounded by the fact that, with decisions taken in Westminster, far from Stormont, people felt that they had little control of their destinies.

There were therefore a strong case for the nascent NIVT and some major problems to be overcome. The long-term strategy envisaged a series of stages and locations for fund-raising (Britain, the Republic, the United States, Europe, etc.), starting with an initial appeal for £500,000. This was not going to be a popular appeal. There is always a problem raising funds for endowment. As the consultants' report said: 'Generally, trusts have been reluctant to provide capital or endowment for other grantmaking trusts and companies might have similar inhibitions.' The strategy aimed to secure the total initial requirement from about 50 sources (therefore at least 150 prospects) with unit targets ranging from £5,000 to £150,000. David Cook has remarked: 'We did not quite use the term at the time but we were in fact pointed in the direction of and moulded into "big-gift" fundraising. And we had a good tutor in our professional consultant.'

There was an important early endorsement and demonstration of support from the Rowntree Trust. This owed much to the imagination and vision of Lewis Waddilove. While the trust deed was being drafted, he advised David Cook on the nature of trusts. He talked to the possible initial trustees about their roles and responsibilities. Then, unasked, within a week of the Trust being formed, he sent £10,000.

After this, progress became difficult. The tactics depended on engaging the attention, then the interest and involvement, of British-based individuals who had origins and links in Northern Ireland and who were in a position either to influence decisions on major blocks of support for the Trust or to establish contacts with such people. The Trust had very few existing contacts of this kind. The trustees without exception had no experience of fund-raising. There was therefore very thorough research into people whose families, education, corporate interests and idealism might predispose them to pay attention. Lord Grey and Lord Longford were among those who gave encouragement and receptions at Westminster for the Trust. Some contacts were made who had time but not the means or influence needed. The process became protracted. This was a difficult time for the trustees.

Then, after eighteen months, Jane Ewart-Biggs (not then a baroness; sadly, she died in 1992) began to work for NIVT. She persuaded Sir David Orr (then Chairman of Unilever), Lord Carr and Sir Brian Corby (then Chairman and Chief Executive of Prudential) to become involved. Sir Fred Catherwood was persuaded to chair a small group formed to lead the Great Britain Appeal Group, which also included Sir Campbell Adamson (Chairman of Abbey National) and Nicholas Horsley (Chairman of Northern Foods). All this preparatory work took the best part of eighteen months.

David Cook said:

In June 1982 we launched our appeal brochure. It was text-book planning: target of £250,000; animated Appeal Group (i.e. good chair and at least two active members); a pyramid of gifts requested ranging from two of £50,000 to fifty of £1,000; systematic research and planning and professional follow-up to all leads. It was quite nail biting, but within ten days of our official launch we were able to announce the lead donations which would set the pace for other donors, even though the big gifts were of course spread over four years.

NIVT more than matched its first £250,000 challenge from government. In 1984, recognising its achievement and the contribution that NIVT was making to community initiatives and cooperation, the government made a new, four-year matching grant arrangement with the Trust. A ceiling of £500,000 was set for this. Jim Prior and Chris Patten were key supporters at this stage.

The appeal in Britain to help match this challenge was launched at the Plaisterer's Hall in London, with support and encouragement from Douglas Hurd, then Secretary of State, and in the presence of the Prince of Wales. Ten days before this function, a major gift of £250,000 was made to the Trust. This gave the trustees confidence to set a £2m appeal target, including the government £500,000 challenge. Guests at the function included previous friends and supporters as well as a new group of prospects identified through systematic research and the Trust's extending network of friends and contacts.

There was a further boost to this £2m appeal when, in June 1986, Tom King as Secretary of State gave a private party, to which David Cook and others from NIVT were invited. The champagne reception was in the old Admiralty building, overlooking the Horse Guards, to watch the Trooping of the Colour. It was a small but financially potent gathering. The rules were clear: there was to be no fund-raising, but a few words were to be said; and of course David Cook could introduce himself and conversation about Northern Ireland and the Trust was not banned. I recall David being very charming and busy with cards and diary, working the rooms.

This was classic big-gift fund-raising, as David Cook has commented. 'We were concentrating our efforts on a small number of people and enterprises who were capable of making large contributions; and we were badgered by Redmond!' But this was not the only fund-raising undertaken. Two radio appeals netted about £9,000. There was a covenant drive. A start was made to the exploration of legacy promotion, a method of giving peculiarly apt for building endowment. There has latterly been some success in attracting 'own-name trusts', where the funds are held and distributed in the settlors' names or in the names of others nominated by them. An outstanding model for this approach is the New York Community Trust, which had been visited by both NIVT and the consultants. Two such own-name trusts have been established to date. One yields an income of £7,000 yearly; the other has provided the Trust with £320,000 capital. With some qualifications about terminology, it can be claimed that NIVT was the forerunner for renewal of community trusts in the United Kingdom (David Cook now chairs ACTAF, the Association of Community Trusts and Foundations).

In March 1990, a further matching grant of £500,000 was negotiated from the government. The 1992 target set by the Trust was £1m, to increase the capital base to £5m. David Cook remarked: 'Ten years on, we now know what to do. It won't be any easier but we now aim to do it on our own.'

Over the years, the pattern of support and grant-making has been as shown in Table 6.2. The situation today is that NIVT has a capital base of £4.25m, generating about £320,000 in revenue. Additionally, over recent years there have been revenue grants from the government of about £200,000 (which in Northern Ireland come through the DHSS) and revenue donations from private sources of about £100,000 yearly. The Trust is currently making grants of about £480,000 yearly.

NIVT was not created simply to raise money. The 1980 consultants' report concluded:

In all this, more will be happening than fund-raising. By involving leaders inside and outside the province in a positive, optimistic programme for the community in Northern Ireland, it is hoped that interest and awareness will be increased and attitudes changed. The characteristics which qualify people for leadership in the programme define them as leaders and influencers of opinion in their own regions. This imposes an unavoidable, additional responsibility on the Trustees.

This is a responsibility that they have embraced effectively. Of course, NIVT has not solved Northern Ireland's fundamental

Table 6.2

Years	1	2	3	4	5	6	7	8	9	10	11	12
Donations to capital												
	10.0	10.0	45.5	96.0	84.0	228.5	171.0	199.0	203.5	500.0	662.0	115.0
Grants made												
	25.5	70.5	70.0	86.0	88.5	108.0	186.0	41.0	397.0	377.0	405.5	481.0

Notes: Capital donations here exclude the matching grant. Figures have been rounded up or down.

problems. 'Nonetheless, drawing on its experience over the past 13 years, the Trust is convinced that community development can make a significant difference to the quality of life of those experiencing poverty and exclusion' (from the NIVT *Five-Year Development Plan*, 1993). Key factors for the future remain poverty in urban and rural communities; communities and sections of society excluded from the mainstream of society; a static economy; no increase in public expenditure; the slow pace of political evolution; continued alienation of those in the most disadvantaged areas. The Trust's grant-making continues to concentrate on 'the most vulnerable and those most at risk of being excluded . . . unattached young people, women's groups, community care, community health, neighbourhood development, and unemployment' as well as the encouragement of community groups 'to explore their art and creativity'. The Trust provides such groups not only with initial funding but also with advice. I know from my other work in the region the extent to which NIVT is looked to for moral support and counsel as well as for funds by organisations throughout Northern Ireland.

Because of NIVT's close awareness of Northern Ireland affairs and relations with community groups, the government has recognised the importance of its approach to community development. A working group of Northern Ireland civil servants was formed in the mid-1980s to look at ways of promoting better community relations there. One outcome of its deliberations was the allocation of £875,000 revenue over five years to NIVT. In the early 1990s, the Trust received £450,000 under the Northern Ireland Public Expenditure Survey. In this area as well, 'The Trust is more than a grant maker and uses its position of independence between government and community groups to seek to inform government on policy and programme matters in relation to the role played by local voluntary and community organisations'.

However, the trustees recognise that to perform a much more adequate and strategic role it must:

- Increase yearly grant-making to £1m.
- Increase its capital base to at least £7.5m.
- Use additional statutory funds (say, £500,000) for pilot community projects in Northern Ireland.

The Trust will look for matching statutory grants to create leverage for raising increased funds from the private sector. It hopes to take advantage of the forthcoming reform of the European Union's structural funds. After Maastricht, the combating of social exclusion is a key objective. The Trust has the staff, structures and procedures that should be the product of a well-implemented strategy. It is of interest that a major evaluation report from Coopers & Lybrand in 1992 commented: 'the Trust have the framework and procedures in place to cope with a substantial increase in funding with little or no increase in administrative costs'. (The preceding paragraphs draw on and quote from NIVT's latest *Five-Year Development Plan*.)

So the fund-raising goes on. There have been changes in the Trust's dedicated and supportive trustees. Hugh Frazer went to Dublin to direct the Combat Poverty Agency and was succeeded in 1988 by his deputy, Paul Sweeney. David Cook remains as Chairman and I leave the final words to him.

Here are his reflections:

- It would be difficult to overestimate the leverage value of the matching grant system. Not only, of course, has it contributed to the capital fund directly but it has also proved an effective attraction to donors to be able to say that their contribution will be matched pound for pound by government.
- Over the past twelve years the Trust has spent £110,000 on fund-raising expenses. Sometimes you have to take a chance. Our 1984 Plaisterer's Hall reception alone cost £6,000 to organise. The line between taking a chance and rational investment can be very thin. You've got to spend money to raise money.

- The basic concept or philosophy of the project you are raising money for has to be good. You've got to believe in it. If you don't, you'll not convince others. Trustees or managers chosen only for their supposed fund-raising ability may not, paradoxically, be the best people to do so.
- You need to build up a track record of achievement in grant-making or good service, depending on your core activities, before you start fund-raising.
- Be clear about the relationship between client and professional fund-raising consultant. The consultant doesn't raise money for you. He or she will create a climate for you in which fund-raising is possible and will educate you, but you, basically, have to do the leg work.
- Understanding the networks of the world of corporate giving is crucial. Research is essential. You may have to invest in taking *The Financial Times*. Time spent in reconnoitring is seldom wasted.
- If you see your potential donors as merely targets, you may well miss the target. In many cases we now have relationships with donors spreading over several years. We have developed a mutual respect for each other. They have in a real sense become our partners.
- It is as much an art as it is a science. By careful research and preparation you can plan your own luck. But you must also learn the art of the rolling conversation.
- It's a serious business and requires a dedicated approach but there has to be some scope for fun also. At least a small proportion of the £110,000 has been spent in Bubbles Wine Bar in Lower Audley Street.

Notes

Chapter 1

This history is more fully treated in my *Wealth of Christians*, Orbis, USA, 1984, *passim*.

1. 1 Corinthians 16. 1–4; 2 Corinthians 8. 16–21.
2. Cf. Emil Schurer, *The Jewish People in the Time of Jesus*, Schocken, New York, 1961, p. 288.
3. Cf. Peah 8.7, etc., *The Mishnah*, trans. Herbert Danby, Oxford University Press, 1933; *The Talmud*, trans. H. Polano, Warne, London and New York, 1978, p. 243; C.G. Montefiore and H. Loewe (eds), *A Rabbinic Anthology*, Schocken, 1974, pp. 174–6.
4. *The Talmud*, p. 198; Gittin 5.9, *The Mishnah*, trans. Danby, p. 314; Montefiore and Loewe, *A Rabbinic Anthology*, p. 424.
5. Jacob R. Marcus, *The Jew in the Medieval World*, Atheneum, New York, 1969, pp. 206f and 219.
6. Inscription AD 161–9, in A.R. Hands' *Charities and Social Aid in Greece and Rome*, Thames & Hudson, London, 1968, p. 206.
   I cannot recall my source for Bubwith.
7. Cf. Paul Veyne, *Bread and Circuses*, Allen Lane, London, 1990, pp. 88, 89 and *passim*.
8. Justin, *Apology*, XVII.6.
9. Robert M. Grant, *Early Christianity and Society: Seven Studies*, Harper & Row, London, 1977, p. 135.
10. Tertullian, *Apologeticus*, Loeb, Cambridge, MA and London, 1977, XLII.8.
11. Basil, *Letters*, Loeb, 1928, CXLII and CXLIII.

12. Cf. Hilary Feldman, *Some Aspects of the Christian Reaction to the Tradition of Classical Munificence with Particular Reference to the Works of John Chrysostom and Libanius*, Oxford M.Litt thesis, 1980, pp. 270f; Henry Chadwick, *The Early Christian Church*, Penguin, 1967, p. 58; Peter Brown, *Power and Persuasion in Late Antiquity*, University of Wisconsin Press, 1992, p. 95.
13. Eusebius, *Ecclesiastical History*, Loeb, 1926 and 1932, IV.XXIII; Cyprian, Ep. 62, in J.P. Migne (ed.), *Patrologiae latinae cursus completus*, 221 vols, Paris, 1844–64; Brown, *Power and Persuasion*, p. 96.
14. Quoted in Chadwick, *The Early Christian Church*, p. 157.
15. Brown, *Power and Persuasion, passim*.
16. Eusebius, *Ecclesiastical History*, V.XVIII.
17. Gildas, *De Excidio Britonum*, 66. On date and place of authorship see Nicholas Higham, *Rome, Britain and the Anglo-Saxons*, Seaby, London, 1992, pp. 130 and 160ff.
18. F.W. Maitland, *Equity*, Cambridge University Press, 1932, pp. 23 and 25; and *Constitutional History of England*, Cambridge University Press, 1908, pp. 223ff.
19. *Piers Plowman, Passus* IX and cf. Mullin, *Wealth of Christians*, pp. 109ff.
20. Bishop Stephan, Ep. VIII and IX, Migne, *Patrologiae latinae*.
21. Stephen Murray, *Building of Troyes Cathedral*, Indiana, 1987, cf. especially Appendix C, 'Analyses of the Workshop and Revenues'.
22. 'How a Cathedral was Built in the Fourteenth Century (Milan Cathedral)', in Edmund Bishop, *Liturgica Historica*, Oxford University Press, 1918, pp. 411ff.
23. See *Accounts of the Fabric of Exeter Cathedral, 1279–1353*, ed. and trans. Audrey M. Erskine, Devon and Cornwall Record Society, Torquay, Part 1 1981, Part 2 1983.
24. For Cathedral fund-raising cf. especially Murray, *Building of Troyes Cathedral*; 'Church-building in the Middle Ages', C.R. Cheney, *Medieval Texts and Studies*, Oxford University Press, 1973, pp. 346ff; Roland Recht (ed.), *Les Bâtisseurs des Cathédrales Gothiques*, Editions les Musées de la Ville de Strasbourg, 1989, esp. Wilhelmus Hermanus Vroom, 'La Construction des Cathédrales au Moyen Age: Une Performance Economique', pp. 81ff; Henry Kraus, *Gold was*

the Mortar, Routledge & Kegan Paul, London, 1979, *passim*. For other medieval fund-raising mentioned, cf. Rotha Mary Cray, *The Mediaeval Hospitals of England*, Cass, London, 1966; Center for Medieval and Renaissance Studies, *The Dawn of Modern Banking*, University of California, Yale, 1979, esp. p. 146; and Mullin, *Wealth of Christians*.

25. Cf. Toulmin Smith with Lujo Brentano, *English Gilds: The Original Ordinances of More than One Hundred Early English Gilds*, Early English Text Society/Oxford University Press, 1870, reprinted 1963, *passim*; W.E. Tate, *The Parish Chest*, Cambridge University Press, 1946, *passim*.

26. Michel Rouche on *matricula pauperum*, in *Etudes sur l'Histoire de la Pauvreté (Moyen Age – XVIe siècle)*, ed. Michael Mollat, Publications de la Sorbonne, pp. 788ff and pp. 224ff.

27. J.R. Tanner, *Tudor Constitutional Documents, AD 1485–1603*, Cambridge University Press, 1930, pp. 480f.

28. *Piers Plowman*, e.g. Prologue 66–80; *Canterbury Tales*, General Prologue and prologue to the Pardoner's Tale.

29. Cf. Kraus, *Gold was the Mortar*, p. 142; G.R. Owst, *Preaching in Medieval England*, c. 1350–1450, Russell & Russell, New York, 1965, pp. 103f.

30. Cf. G.R. Elton, *The Reformation 1520–1559*, Cambridge University Press, 1975, pp. 76f; Owen Chadwick, *The Reformation*, Penguin, Harmondsworth, 1972, pp. 41ff; A.G. Dickens, *The English Reformation*, Fontana Collins, Glasgow, p. 94.

31. Tanner, *Tudor Documents*, p. 480.

32. C.F. Pascoe, *Two Hundred Years of the SPG 1701–1900*, SPG, London, 1901, pp. 53, 649, 742, 483, 824; cf. Cray, *Mediaeval Hospitals*, p. 180.

33. John Bellers, 'Proposals for Raising a College of Industry 1696', collected in Hugh Barbour and Arthur O. Roberts, *Early Quaker Writings 1650–1700*, Eerdmans, Grand Rapids, MI, 1973, pp. 451f.

34. W.K. Lowther Clarke, *A History of the SPCK*, SPCK, 1959, pp. 88ff; David Owen, *English Philanthropy 1660 to 1960*, Harvard University Press, 1964, pp. 481ff; and cf. M.G. Jones, *The Charity School Movement*, Cass, Cambridge, 1938, p. 252.

35. Owen, *English Philanthropy*, p. 48.

36. Pascoe, *SPG*, pp. 53, 649, 742, 783.

37. See the paintings and *Messiah* manuscript held by the Thomas Coram Foundation, which is heir to the Foundling Hospital.
38. Quoted in F.K. Prochaska, *Women and Philanthropy in 19th Century England*, Oxford University Press, 1980, p. 60. The Press Bazaar was a fund-raising initiative for the London Hospital which published its own newspaper and used the quoted text as its motto.
39. Owen, *English Philanthropy*, pp. 480f.
40. Cf. Arnaud C. Marts, *Philanthropy's Role in Civilisation*, Harper, 1953, p. 108; Harold J. Seymour, *Designs for Fundraising*, McGraw-Hill, New York, 1966, p. 173; Redmond Mullin, *The Fundraising Handbook*, Mowbrays, Oxford, 1976, pp. 96f.
41. Cf. Pascoe, *SPG*, pp. x, 195, etc.; Robert T.A. Hardy, *A History of the Churches in the United States and Canada*, Oxford University Press, 1976, pp. 278f; Mullin, *Wealth of Christians*, pp. 115ff and 147ff.
42. Mullin, *Wealth of Christians*, pp. 180ff.
43. Cf. Marion Allford, *Charity Appeals: The Complete Guide to Success*, Dent, 1992.
44. See Select bibliography.

Chapter 2

1. There is a related discussion in Redmond Mullin, *Present Alms: On the Corruption of Philanthropy*, Phlogiston, Birmingham, 1980, pp. 8ff.
2. Personal recollection.
3. Redmond Mullin, *Arts, Initiative and Money*, Gulbenkian, AIMS, London, 1984, pp. 19, 37f and *passim*.
4. Barry Knight, *Voluntary Action*, Centre for Research and Innovation in Social Policy and Practice (CENTRIS), Home Office, 1993.

Chapter 3

1. Redmond Mullin, *The Fundraising Cycle*, Redmond Mullin Ltd, 1987.

2. Mullin, *Present Alms*, p. 3.
3. See Susanna Hoe, *Scott Bader: The Man who Gave His Company Away*, Heinemann, 1978.

Chapter 4

1. A tape was published by the Institute of Fundraising Managers.
2. Derived from Redmond Mullin, *Marketing Covenants*, Redmond Mullin Ltd, 1988.

Chapter 5

1. For a discussion of increasing-returns economics by Brian Arthur and others at the Santa Fe Institute, see M. Mitchell Waldrop, *Complexity*, Viking, London and New York, 1993, esp. pp. 34–6.
2. Quoted from Roger Lewin, *Complexity*, Phoenix, London, 1993, pp. 12–13.

Select bibliography

Allford, Marion, *Charity Appeals: The Complete Guide to Success,* Dent in association with ICFM, 1992: an account of the Wishing Well Appeal

Burnett, Ken, *Relationship Fundraising,* White Lion Press, 1992: a practical and inspiring text on relationship fund-raising

Chesterman, Michael, *Charities, Trusts and Social Welfare,* Weidenfeld & Nicolson, 1979: contains some historical material

Clarke, Sam, *The Complete Fundraising Handbook,* The Directory of Social Change in association with ICFM, 1992: detailed and workmanlike

Drucker, Peter, *Managing the Non-Profit Organisation,* Butterworth-Heinemann, Oxford, 1990

Kotler, Philip and Andreasen, Alan, *Strategic Marketing for Nonprofit Organizations,* Prentice Hall, 1991: a classic text updated

Mullin, Redmond, *Present Alms: On the Corruption of Philanthropy,* Phlogiston, Birmingham, 1980: explores principles and ways ahead for the sector

Mullin, Redmond, *The Wealth of Christians,* Orbis, USA, 1984: includes more extensive study of the sector's history since the beginning of the Christian era

Mullin, Redmond, *Arts, Initiative and Money,* Gulbenkian, AIMS, London, 1984

Picarda, Hubert, *The Law and Practice Relating to Charities,* Butterworths, 1977

Stones, Helena, Catherine McCarthy and Hendrik Ball (eds), *The Giving Business*, BBC (Business Matters), London, 1990: a series of papers from two Martyn Lewis programmes including Marion Allford on the Wishing Well Appeal and Redmond Mullin on strategic fund-raising

ICFM: Guidance Notes and Standard Form of Contract for dealing with Consultants
Code of Practice on Lotteries
Code of Practice on Reciprocal Mailing
Code of Practice on Schools
Code of Practice on Telephone Recruitment of Collectors
Code of Practice on House-to-House Collections
Draft Code of Practice: Static Collection Boxes
Draft Code of Practice: Outbound Telephone Support

Index